LAYERS
of
STITCH

This small panel was based on wall paintings in the Sainte-Chapelle, Paris. Nappy (diaper) liner was applied to cotton and then decorated with fabrics and automatic patterns. Stitched acanthus leaves with burned edges were added as patches. The borders were made from computer-printed, hand-made paper.

LAYERS

of

STITCH

VAL CAMPBELL-HARDING

MAGGIE GREY

B T BATSFORD

Acknowledgements

We would like to thank all our colleagues and students who have loaned work for this book and Michael Wicks for his excellent photography. We would also like to thank Clive for all the computer work and the following sewing machine manufacturers for all their help: Bernina, Brother, Husqvana-Viking, Janome and Pfaff.

First published 2001
This edition published 2004

Text and designs © Valerie Campbell-Harding and Maggie Grey 2000, 2004

The right of Valerie Campbell-Harding and Maggie Grey to be identified as Authors of this work has been asserted by them in accordance with the Copyright, Designs and Patents Act 1998
Photography by Michael Wicks

ISBN 0 7134 8906 5

A CIP catalogue record for this book is available from the British Library.

Printed and bound in Singapore
for the publishers
BT Batsford
Chrysalis Books Group
The Chrysalis Building
Bramley Road
London W10 6SP

www.batsford.com

An imprint of **Chrysalis** Books Group plc

Contents

Introduction

This is an exciting time for machine embroiderers. Today's sewing machines, with their decorative patterns, memory functions, embroidery cards, scanners and software, have dramatically increased the potential for embroidery. New machines and products are appearing all the time, and machine embroidery continues to develop and evolve to take advantage of these innovations.

This book aims to encourage not only new ways of decorating fabric by painting, distressing and stitching but also the use of some of the wide variety of machine feet that will create unusual effects. In addition, it looks at exciting ways of incorporating and extending the patterns, letters and stitches that are built into sewing machines and considers the creative use of commercial embroidery cards and sewing machine scanners and of the software that drives sewing machines.

When we began working with computerized machines, we found that we fell naturally into a way of working that had proved its worth throughout time: the making of patches or motifs to apply to a prepared, usually stitched, background. This is the approach we have adopted in this book, which is divided into four parts: backgrounds, stitched motifs, applying the motifs to backgrounds and finishing techniques. The book describes each process in a step-by-step way and offers lots of new and imaginative methods of machine embroidery.

The wide range of materials used brings a mixed media element to our work and encouraged us to find new ways of stitching with them. Combining methods has led us to break down boundaries, and the resulting stitchery is used in weaving and three-dimensional forms. Many embroiderers find that finishing their work causes problems, and these aspects are fully covered in the final part of this book.

Because it takes the design aspects of machine embroidery into account, the organization of this book – the making of separate backgrounds and motifs and then combining them in finished pieces – stretches the imagination and offers new avenues for exploration.

MATERIALS AND EQUIPMENT

Although it is perfectly possible to tackle all the pieces described in this book by using a basic sewing machine for free machine embroidery, we have included descriptions of the new generation of sewing machines, with their scanning devices and controlling software. These machines, which can translate your own drawings into stitch, need to be used imaginatively so that the results look spontaneous and natural.

Among the other equipment that can be invaluable for these pieces are the heat guns or heating tools that are used by rubber stampers to heat embossing powders, which can have a magical effect on some fabrics, and that would be a worthwhile investment. Soldering irons can be used to distress stitched motifs or to carve shapes into velvets, sheer fabrics or polycottons. Remember to protect surfaces with an old metal tray before using a soldering iron. If you use either of these tools it is worth getting a mask or respirator; these are widely available and are not expensive.

The range of colouring media grows all the time. We have found some new uses for old favourites, including Markal oil sticks and bronze (metallic) powders, and we have also tried out some new ones, such as ChromaCoal, a chalky pastel in stick form that can be heat-set on fabric. The range of metallic paints is also increasing rapidly, offering new opportunities for creating glistening or pearly surfaces, and embossing powders, of the kind used by rubber stampers, have a lot to offer, too; these are available in good craft shops. Water-soluble paper and puff paints, such as Xpandaprint (which produces a three-dimensional surface when it is heated), provide ways of adding texture, and we have even explored the potential of using humble nappy (diaper) liners, bought from a well-known chain of chemists.

A temporary fixing agent, such as 505 Spray, can be extremely useful if you are applying a fabric or motifs to a background. The adhesive will hold them together for just long enough for you to stitch them but will not harm the materials.

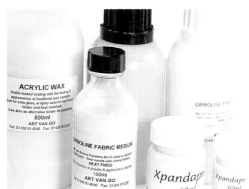

You will probably already have a good stock of materials in your store cupboard, so try those before rushing out to buy more.

Chapter One

Backgrounds

1. Paint and Texture

A black fabric was partially bleached, then painted with dilute silk paint. Close stitching was worked over the whole piece to blend the painted shapes.

There are many ways of creating backgrounds for embroideries. Take a piece of fabric, add colour – with paint, oil sticks, tea or coffee, if you wish – apply further fabric (or even paper) to it, texture it, use layering and burning techniques ... the possibilities are many and exciting. Stitching can also be used to decorate the background fabric, and the sewing machine feet and attachments, many of which are supplied with the machines, can be used, too.

Just as exciting as the processes are the fabrics that are available. In addition to traditional cottons, silks and velvets, there are scrim, silk papers and vanishing muslin. New materials are appearing all the time: dissolvable paper and wire-mesh (which can be stitched) can be combined with such unlikely sounding items as nappy (diaper) liners and newspaper.

A good background should add colour, texture and interest, but take care that it doesn't become too busy or overpower the patches and motifs that are to be placed on it.

Painted Bondaweb was ironed on to calico to make a background.

PAINTING FABRIC

Silk or fabric paints can be used as a base for many paint techniques. It can also be useful to get into the habit of making a stencil for each design source you work on from the special plastic that is sold for stencil making. Use one of the pens that are used for overhead projector slides to trace the design, then cut out the motif with a craft knife or use an electric stencil cutter. Although it is delicate, transparency film (acetate), of the kind used for overhead projectors, can also be used for stencils, which are used in many of the techniques described in this book.

PAINTING BONDAWEB

Bondaweb is the proprietary name of an iron-on fusible bonding web, which is used to fuse fabrics together in appliqué work. Because of the way the backing is attached, however, when it is painted, it becomes extremely textural. Painted Bondaweb can be ironed on the fabric or paper as a colouring medium without having a piece of fabric on top. It may feel a little sticky after ironing, but the tackiness will disappear within a day or so.

Decorate some Bondaweb with silk paint or diluted acrylic paint and leave to dry. Spraying a little water on the Bondaweb before you begin will help the colours to merge. The Bondaweb can then be ironed on to a piece of plain or coloured fabric to add colour and texture. Ironing sheer fabrics over the top will soften the effect. More exciting results can be obtained by ironing the Bondaweb over a fabric that has been decorated with gold paint or Markal oil sticks. Try

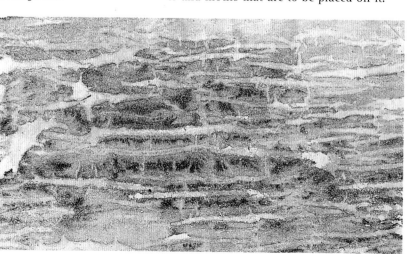

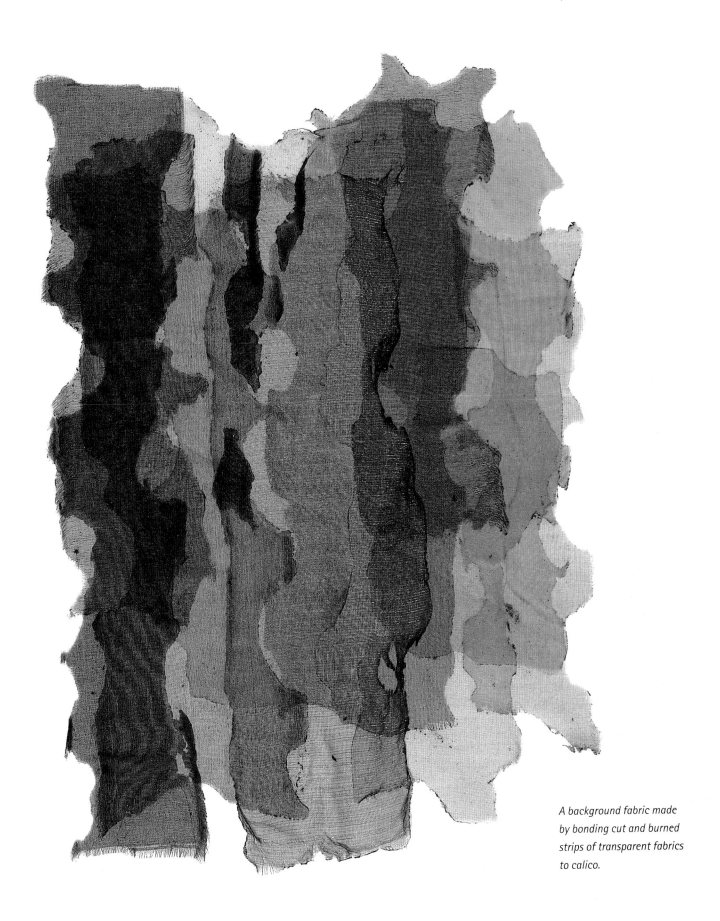

A background fabric made by bonding cut and burned strips of transparent fabrics to calico.

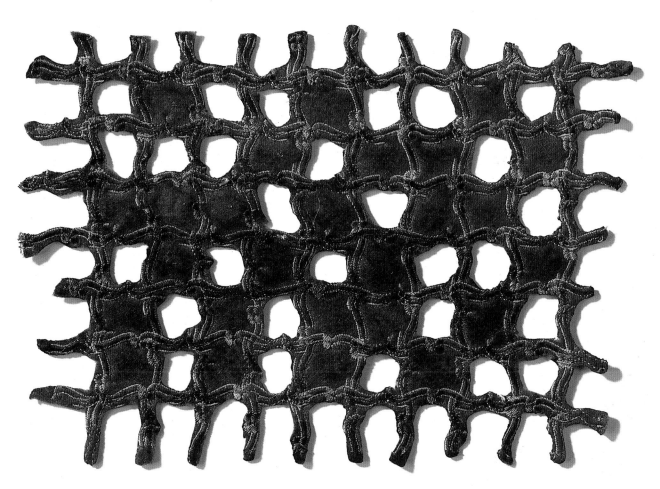

using Bondaweb with the zapping techniques described on page 38.

Ironing painted Bondaweb on to paper, especially paper that has been gilded or treated with melted wax or Markal oil sticks, gives excellent results. The paper can be painted and then crumpled to add texture. When you iron over crumpled paper, work with a light touch on the iron or the crinkles will be smoothed out. Apply a hot iron for just long enough to transfer the Bondaweb to the paper, then carefully peel back the paper, pushing back any Bondaweb that is reluctant to leave it. Brown paper can be especially effective when it is treated in this way, and if you wish it can be block printed or computer printed first. Adding some gold acrylic paint on top, using an almost dry brush to avoid 'splodges', will pick up the texture of the webbing. The paper should be backed with fabric – calico or something similar – before stitching. Use spray adhesive to give a permanent bond.

PAINTING STITCHING

Interesting effects can be achieved if you stitch first and add colour afterwards. Take a pale background fabric and stitch all over it using built-in patterns, motifs from an embroidery unit or free machine embroidery. A pale coloured thread – cotton, rayon or similar – will take the colour well. When the stitching is complete, paint the entire piece, stitching and all, with silk or fabric paints. You can use acrylic paints, but they will make the fabric feel stiffer and will need to be vigorously brushed into the surface. When the paint is dry apply some acrylic wax, using it straight from the bottle or

ABOVE
Twin-needle stitching, worked using an automatic pattern, was cut out, holes were cut in it, and it was then coloured using transfer paint.

OPPOSITE
This small panel, with a background of Xpandaprint and automatic patterns, was painted after stitching. Cut-out felt, with zigzag shapes, was applied.

mixing in metallic powders to add golden highlights. Remember to wear a mask when you use gold powders so that you do not breathe in the particles. Markal oil sticks can also be used; simply rub the stick lightly over the surface to highlight the stitching

Transfer paints can also be used to colour pre-stitched pieces. Apply the paint to the paper as usual and then iron this on to stitched fabric. The fabric and the thread should be synthetic – polyester, rayon or any other manmade fabric – and metallic threads work particularly well. Do not limit yourself to white material: some of the coloured synthetics give excellent results, so experiment with the poly-velvets, poly-silks, poly-satins, poly-wools or poly-linens.

Try winding heavy threads, even fine jap gold thread, on to the bobbin and then work upside down. Stitched motifs or machine embroidery will create unusual effects when the colour from the paper is ironed over them because they raise the stitched area and can leave interesting voids in the fabric beneath the stitching.

ADDING TEXTURE
Puff Paints
Puff paint products, such as Xpandaprint, can be an exciting way to add texture to fabric. The products can be used simply by sponging or brushing a little (do not be too generous) on to fabric. Choose a fabric that does not have too much surface texture and use a heat gun or iron on the back of the fabric to puff up the paint. If you wish, the resulting textured background can be painted with silk, fabric or acrylic paint.

Puff Paint Stencils
Sponge Xpandaprint through a stencil or doily on to a piece of smooth fabric and leave it until it is completely dry. Stitch words, letters or automatic patterns in a random fashion on top of the dry Xpandaprint, using metallic thread and large stitches, then heat with an iron on the reverse of the fabric or use a heat gun on the right side to puff the Xpandaprint. This can then be decorated with silk or fabric paints. Acrylic paints can also be used, and these often give better coverage. The paint will cover some of the text too, but most should still show through. You really need to push the paint into the Xpandaprint with a stiff brush.

Make some home-made wax (mix 1 teaspoon of hard silicon furniture polish with $\frac{1}{2}$ teaspoon of bronze powder and remember to wear a mask when using the powder) or use something like Treasure Gold Wax and rub it lightly on to the raised areas of the piece. Although we have used it as a background, this is a good technique on its own for items like book covers, cushions and bags.

Nappy Liners
Another good way to texture a background is to apply nappy (diaper) liners to it. When heat is applied with an iron or a heat gun the liners melt into the fabric and, if you wish, can carry colour and pattern. We have found that the best results are achieved with liners from a well-known chain of chemists and that other brands do not always dissolve, but experiment for yourself. Try the following method on a pale coloured, smooth fabric.

1   Place the nappy (diaper) liner over a textured surface – a metal mesh or a series of printing blocks, for example – and rub with a Markal oil stick. Do not be too precise if you are using blocks, and rub parts of the block rather then regular prints. Work with small pieces at first.

Xpandaprint was dabbed all over a piece of fabric and painted with fabric paints. A little gold foil was added in places, and the whole piece was stitched to integrate it.

2 Lay the fabric on an ironing board, place the nappy (diaper) liner, Markal side up, on top, cover it with baking parchment and iron with a hot iron. When the 'white' of the liner disappears, pull off the baking parchment. (This does not always work because some irons just do not get hot enough.) Place another piece of liner next to it and repeat the process.

3 When the fabric is covered, decorate it with silk paint or runny fabric paint. The texture will resemble that of an old wall. If you want, lightly apply some metallic wax with a fingertip. The same method can be used with smooth black fabric as a base. Again, if too much white is left, it can be painted, although most of the white will have disappeared.

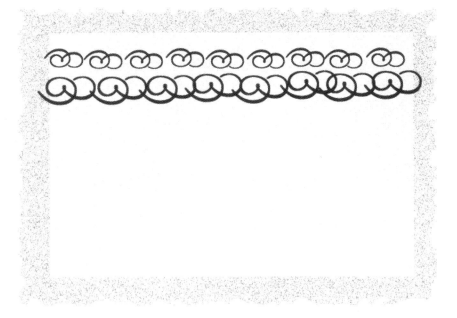

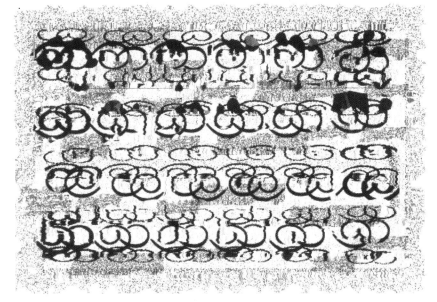

Nappy (diaper) liners can also be applied to cheap, stretchy, acrylic velvet. The liner is decorated with oil stick and applied to the fabric, which is then stretched. This gives a wonderfully cracked and distressed fabric. Stretch the fabric over a firm base, pin it down and stitch with lines of decorative patterns. These will partly sink into the velvet, but this can be exploited by further stitching over strips of water-soluble fabric (which can be later washed away with cold water). The water-soluble fabric will keep the stitching on the top of the pile, which gives an interesting effect.

A nappy (diaper) liner that has been rubbed with an oil stick can be stitched to a backing fabric by means of built-in patterns. Lines of lettering also work well. When the stitching is complete, apply a heat gun to the liner. Ironing the stitched, nappy-linered fabric before heating it would give yet another effect.

The backgrounds could be further enhanced by couching down strips of fabric or threads. Applying strips of sheer fabric – holding them in place by using built-in patterns and piling pattern on pattern – would produce a richly decorated surface. The fabric made by this method should be washable (provided that the paints were heat-set), and it could be used for clothing or cushions as well as for making a good background to a wall-hanging.

Fig. 1

Nappy (diaper) liner is laid on a fabric and stitched with lines of pattern (top). After stitching, a heat gun is used to melt away much of the liner and give an informal look to the stitching (bottom).

A small book was made with a cover created from fabric with heat-treated nappy (diaper) liner, with free machining and beads.

2. Appliqué for Backgrounds

Fig. 2
Shapes can be cut from a variety of fabrics, bonded or pinned to a background and secured with lines of straight, free running stitches or patterned stitching.

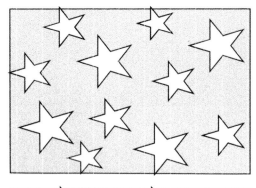

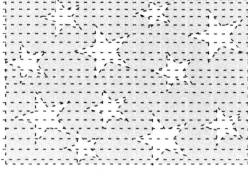

BELOW
The background fabric was made by covering calico with pieces of transparent material in different colours. It was decorated with applied stitched patches and strips of zigzag paper, and the whole was then covered with lines of straight stitching.

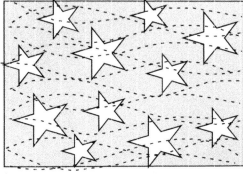

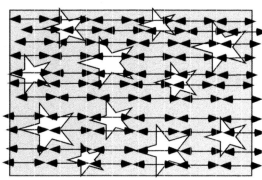

APPLIED SHAPES

Shapes can be cut from fabric or paper and applied to a background fabric, possibly one that has been previously painted or textured. Cut out the shapes and use a low-tack adhesive spray, such as 505, to hold them to the backing fabric. Stitch all over to integrate them with the background. The stitching can be simple lines of straight stitching or you can use pattern stitches. The colour of the thread you use is important, and usually thread that is slightly darker than the background is most effective. Alternatively, you could use bands of colour, perhaps shading from light to dark, on both the background and the shapes and a thread that also changes in tone as it crosses the fabric.

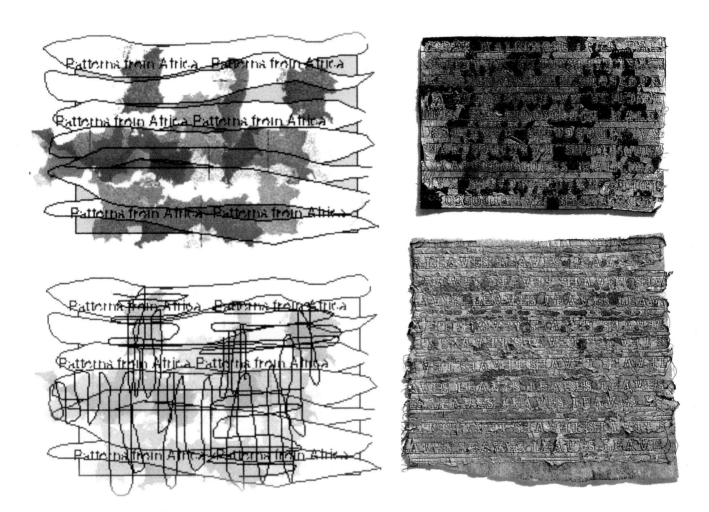

NEWSPAPER

The next group of backgrounds exploit the memory options of your sewing machine. Put a phrase of text into the memory. The number of words you use will depend on the memory capacity of your machine, and you might find that you have to store a series of words in separate memories; check the manual for your machine for detailed instructions.

Sponge a sheet of newspaper with tea or coffee, allow it to dry and spray with black or gold webbing spray (available from embroidery suppliers or hobby shops), which gives a wonderful, cracked appearance to the surface. Place the paper over a background fabric and stitch your chosen phrase, repeating a word or words, all over the paper. You can vary the pattern by working in bands, with decorative patterns at the top and bottom of each band. If your machine has a text option that gives outlined letters you can get excellent results. When you have finished, scrub the surface with a hard bristle or wire brush. Lots of the paper will come away, leaving a lovely soft-textured, distressed surface.

If you wish you can extend the technique by painting some Bondaweb with acrylic, silk or runny paints (spray with water first). When it is completely dry, iron the Bondaweb on to a piece of felt. Proceed with the newspaper as before, but do not iron the paper to the

TOP LEFT **Fig. 3**

Strips of newspaper laid over a background are secured with lines of letters or patterns and free running stitches. The newspaper is dampened and then rubbed away to break up the regularity and reveal more of the background fabric.

ABOVE

Fabric from newspaper. The top sample was made with black felt as the base, and the lower sample with white felt, dyed with coffee. Both samples were coloured with dilute silk paint.

Acrylic-painted Bondaweb was ironed on to felt, and newspaper was stitched and distressed to form borders.

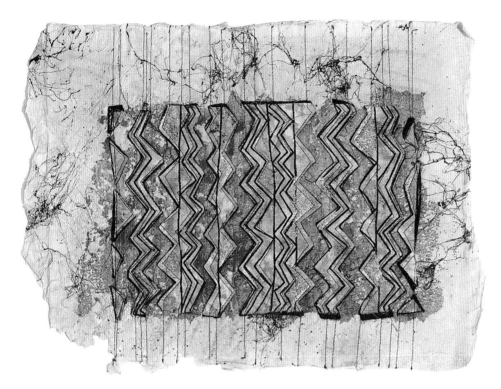

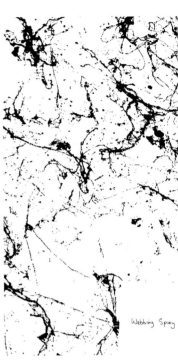

Bondaweb, just place it on top. Alternatively, use velvet to which nappy (diaper) liner has been applied instead of felt.

Water-soluble paper can be used instead of newspaper. Stitch the water-soluble paper in the same way as newspaper, but when you have finished stitching, paint some areas with nail varnish. These painted areas will not wash away. Pin the fabric to a polystyrene tile or something similar and hold it under a slow-running tap. The paper that is not protected by the nail varnish will quickly be washed away. Blot the piece gently with kitchen paper and leave it to dry, which will take some time. An alternative effect can be achieved by not applying the varnish resist but just giving a quick squirt of water to the surface. Paint it when it is dry.

TISSUE PAPER

Ordinary tissue paper can be bonded to a background fabric to give an effective surface for paints, especially when the colour is bleached out. Any drawing or painting media can be used on the tissue paper before it is bonded to the fabric, or it can be coloured afterwards.

Cut a piece of tissue paper to size. Use Bondaweb with an iron (do not use a damp cloth) to fix it to calico, craft iron-on interfacing (Vilene) or felt, ironing the Bondaweb to the background and peeling off the paper first. Then crumple the tissue paper slightly as it is placed on the warm surface to give a more interesting texture before ironing through silicone paper to fix the tissue paper to the background. Computer-printed tissue paper can also be used: attach a piece of tissue paper to ordinary printing paper with low-tack adhesive spray or Pritt stick around the edges and put it through the printer (note that it may not be light fast, however).

The resulting fabric can be sponged with tea or coffee and allowed to dry before being sprayed with webbing spray, which make it look like old parchment. Wax can then be

Fig. 4

Webbing spray on fabric looks rather like the fine veins in marble.

TOP LEFT

Painted Bondaweb was ironed on to calico, which was dyed with coffee, covered with tissue paper and sprayed with webbing spray. Strips of chevron-patterned fabric, backed with felt and embroidered, were cut out and applied with additional stitching.

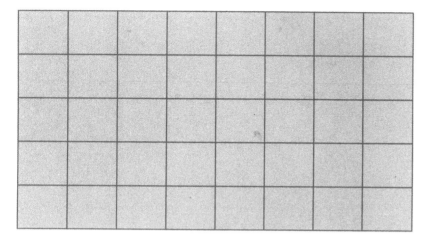

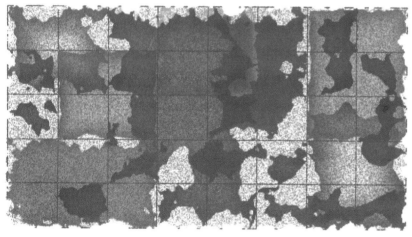

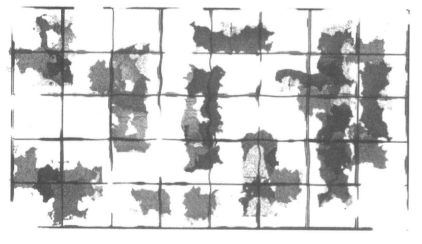

Fig. 5

If painted vanishing muslin is stitched in a grid pattern (top)
and then heated with a heat gun (centre), tattered and torn
fragments will be left (bottom).

applied to the fabric, and a gold encaustic wax (made from beeswax), which gives a translucent gleam, is especially effective on this type of surface. Button polish, on the other hand, gives a deep, shiny, chestnut-like surface.

Another colouring method is to use silk paints. Allow them to dry and then paint the surface with an ink, such as Quink, that will react to bleach. When the ink is dry, dab the surface lightly with a sponge dipped in bleach and the ink will disappear, revealing the silk paint beneath.

Stencils also work well on tissue paper, especially when they are combined with the ink and bleach method.

VANISHING MUSLIN

This fine fabric is usually stitched to a background and then heated with an iron or a heat gun, when it will disappear. Interesting effects can be obtained by painting or tea-dyeing it and then heating a few areas to give a frayed and distressed appearance. Place a piece of spare fabric under the muslin to absorb surplus paint and decorate it with silk paints or fabric paints, which are fast when heated. Allow the paint to dry naturally and do not use heat to hasten the process. The muslin can then be stitched with machine embroidery or an embroidery unit, which can be fitted to some sewing machines. If you use a unit, it is probably sensible to use two layers. Do not pull up too tightly into the frame or the muslin will tear.

Alternatively, the muslin could be laid on a prepared background, held in place with a stitched grid and then heated away. The stitched lines will retard the heating process, leaving the grid revealed. Alternatives to a grid would be stitched lines of built-in

Painted vanishing muslin was applied to black felt over stitched patches. More stitching was worked, and then a heat gun was used to dissolve the muslin.

pattern or letters, but whichever you choose, the fabric can then be distressed by heating. Another approach would be to stencil the fabric, and embroidery could be used to echo and enhance the stencil. Couching threads could be tacked by hand within the stencil and machine embroidered to add density. Stitch into the couching thread using free-machine techniques and then machine lightly outside the stencilled area.

When stitching is complete, place the muslin between sheets of baking parchment and iron until some parts begin to disappear, or use a heat gun. The muslin will darken and become crumbly but take care not to overdo it or too much will vanish. Pull at the edges with your fingers to encourage frayed edges. The resulting fabric can then be applied to a background, used as a border or stitched in strips to a background to add texture.

Distressed Effects with Vanishing Muslin

Vanishing muslin can be used to create a range of distressed effects on fabric. Take a piece of felt or fabric backing and place on it pieces of fabric, cut pieces of stitching or patches and motifs. Pieces of painted vanishing muslin, not yet dissolved, should also be added. Stitch spaced lines of words or patterns across the fabric with lines of straight stitch between them. Note that close stitching will prevent more of the muslin from being dissolved away, thus leaving more attached to the backing fabric. Heat the surface with a heat gun and then rub the muslin away with a toothbrush, soft wire brush or even your fingernail.

This base fabric can be lightly painted with gold paint (use acrylic or fabric paint mixed with metallic powders). Alternatively, add more motifs or another layer of vanishing muslin (which could be a grid as before). More stitching will be needed to attach the pieces and blend them in.

Spray low-tack adhesive over some backing fabric and place a piece of painted fabric over the backing. Use stencils (see page 10) to apply fabric paints to the painted fabric, then grate wax crayons over it, place silicon paper on top and melt it with an iron.

For a different effect iron a piece of painted Bondaweb over the entire piece, cover it with a sheet of silicon paper and then, using a medium iron, stick cut pieces of foil to the surface to emphasize the design. Place pieces of heated, painted, vanishing muslin informally over the design. Consider the colour implications of this addition. Lay cut-out patches over the piece, positioning them carefully to enhance the pattern, and then cover the whole thing with a layer of chiffon. Stitch all over, using straight or open pattern stitches, to secure the layers. Finally, apply heat to the chiffon with a heat gun.

3. Stitched Backgrounds

Adding stitches to a fabric affects not only the way it looks but also the way it feels and the way it reacts to being handled. Stitching, even straight lines, can be used to add colour, texture and surface interest to a piece of work, and this can be demonstrated by working some built-in patterns or letters on a fine fabric, such as lawn or polycotton, without using a stabilizer. The fabric will pucker and will take on an almost smocked appearance.

In general, however, a stabilizer of some kind will be needed for most stitch applica-

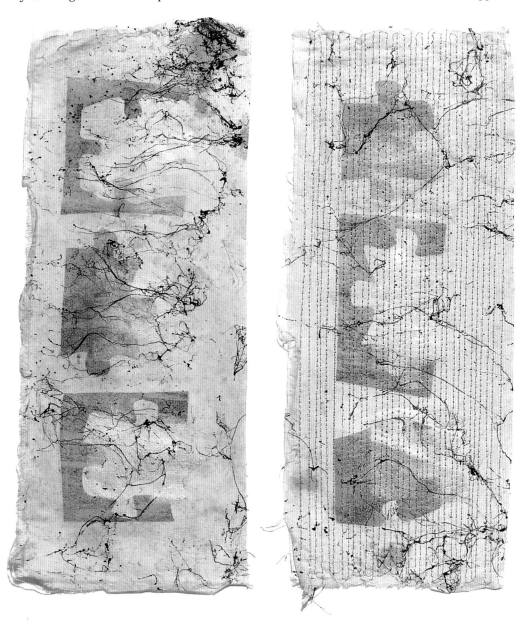

Calico was dyed with coffee and stencilled with first red, then gold fabric paint. One piece was covered with lines of straight stitching.

Velvet with applied nappy (diaper) liner was covered with straight lines of automatic patterns, some raised using water-soluble fabric. Motifs from a Brother card were stitched on water-soluble paper and net, and some resist was applied before the water-soluble paper was dissolved. It was then decorated with metallic paints.

OPPOSITE

Lines of straight stitching and lettering were worked on scrunched dyed cotton.

tions, and there are many kinds to choose from. Water-soluble stabilizers, which can be washed away to leave only the fabric and the stitches, are ideal for use with fine or sheer fabrics. Tear-away stabilizers can be detached from the fabric, leaving only a trace behind the stitching. Iron-on interfacing can be used to back fabrics; choose a weight that is appropriate for the material used. Felt, calico and cheap polycotton can also be used.

Heavy stitching, in the form of pattern over pattern or a heavy build-up of machine embroidery, will distort fabric and pull it out of shape, which can be a nuisance or can be made into a feature of the work. Some sewing machine software has an under-stitching function to counteract this pulled effect, and this is considered on page 75.

Using two threads in the needle gives added weight to the stitching and can sometimes add texture if one thread loops slightly. Most machines will accept two threads quite easily, so think about mixing colours: using a plain thread with a variegated one, or a metallic with a plain one and so on. Two threads will also provide denser cover to stitching, and the contrast between light and heavy threads can be attractive because it alters the way the light reflects from the work.

Built-in patterns look wonderful on velvet. They tend to sink into the pile, so use fairly heavy satin stitch patterns. These will not be obvious, so place strips of water-soluble fabric over the velvet and stitch patterns on them. This approach will keep the stitches above the velvet and produce

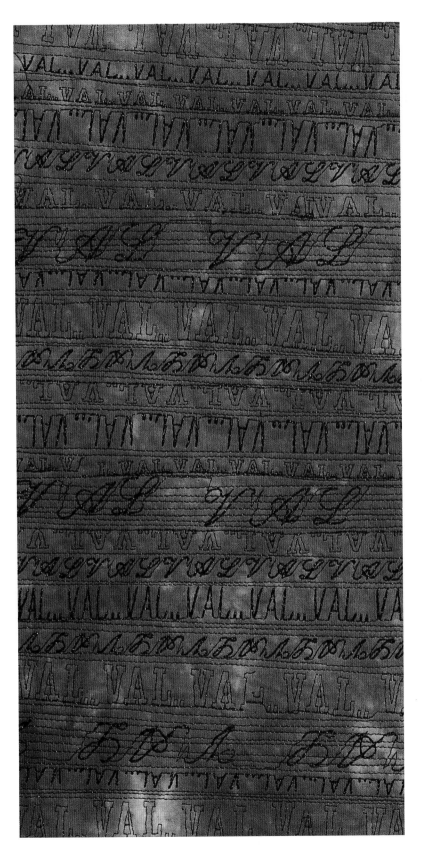

Fig. 6
Stitch density can be altered by using thinner or thicker threads or two or even three threads through the needle.

A pattern enlarged in Pfaff 7570 software was stitched in lines on painted calico with thread of different thicknesses to create variation. Some was worked from the back in reverse whip stitch, using a much looser top tension, to give added weight.

A pattern enlarged in the Pfaff 7570 software was stitched in lines on painted calico. The same pattern, worked on black felt and cut out, was knotted and applied on top.

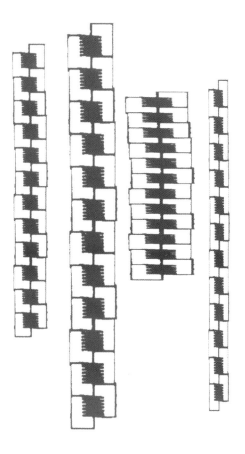

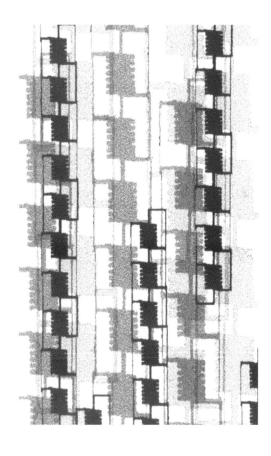

Fig. 7
Built-in sewing machine patterns can be enlarged in the software, and using different sizes together will create variety.

interesting 'over and under' effects. Use cold water to dissolve the fabric when you have finished. Do not overlook simple solutions such as changing the weight of the thread to alter the appearance of the stitching. The density of the thread has a great influence on the pattern and thus the texture of the work.

If your machine does not like using two threads in the needle, use them in the bobbin. It is possible to use multiple threads in the bobbin, but they will probably have to be wound by hand. Heavy threads look good on the bobbin, especially some of the space-dyed, hand-stitch threads.

Couching a heavier thread by using machine embroidery or built-in patterns is another option. A braiding, or pearls and piping, foot can be useful for this.

ENLARGING BUILT-IN PATTERNS

Some machines have software to enlarge built-in patterns or to construct large patterns that can be stitched with the embroidery unit in place. If you have a Pfaff the built-in patterns can be enlarged and stitched with the foot on; if you have another type of machine work with the embroidery unit in place.

Open patterns will alter the way a fabric handles and give more body. They also imitate a woven fabric, add background texture and change the colour or tone of the fabric. Satin stitch patterns can be cut out and applied to a background, or they can be used to make a rich, heavy, jacquard-type fabric, which is ideal for bags or purses. Use the enlarged patterns in the following ways:

- Couch strips of fabric, threads or strips of cut-up stitching.

- Mix different sizes together; the change of scale and density produces an interesting effect.
- Stitch on water-soluble fabric.
- Stitch as a grid, with open spaces.
- Swing the fabric as you stitch to distort the stitch.
- Use a printed fabric and stitch the same motif.
- Build up a mass of lines or squiggles.
- Outline patterns with free running stitch or satin stitch.
- Cut out shapes and apply them to a stitched background, wrap around a cord or knot loosely.
- Use the techniques described for painted stitches (see page 13) – for example, stitch cream on cream and then ink and bleach.

ENLARGING AND DISTORTING PATTERNS ON THE PFAFF

If you have Pfaff software load in the numbered patterns. Using Maxi mode, change the size to whatever you wish. Try Times 2, 3 or even larger. You can keep the same proportions or change them to distort the pattern. Send the new pattern back to P-memory on the sewing machine and stitch it. The memory has a lot of capacity and will store many patterns. Patterns can also be stored on the computer. All these effects look good if they are worked with variegated threads.

Remember that you will need to use a backing fabric or stabilizer. Do not stitch too fast if you are using a tricky (rayon or metallic) thread or it will break. Use foot no. 8, but because the patterns are more open, a thicker thread (30) can be used.

Keeping the lines of stitching straight can be difficult, so draw lines (you can only check this between patterns because the pattern is wider than the foot and the machine moves

around so much), use the quilting guide or do it by eye and do not bother about being too accurate. Some patterns start at one corner and others in the centre, so stitch some samples to find out which method applies.

Try the following: stitch in lines or short bursts, moving the fabric between bursts, or in curves. Both 9mm (3/8in) and large patterns can be loaded from the Pfaff into the software, details isolated and parts of the pattern enlarged or distorted using Maxi mode. This is quite different from combining patterns in the sewing machine memory, when you can use only the complete patterns.

Details of two or three different patterns can be highlighted, copied and pasted into each other, either at the end or in the middle of a pattern, to make dozens of combinations.

Individual sections can be highlighted and then moved nearer to or further away from each other using the 'move' tool. Any highlighted section can be mirrored or flipped. These are often most effective if they are widened rather then just enlarged in proportion, and then downloaded back into the P-memory of the sewing machine.

Fig. 8
Three Maxi patterns.

Material with applied painted tissue paper, stitched with enlarged Maxi patterns.

Fig. 9
Larger or Maxi patterns already on the sewing machine can be combined with 9mm (3/8in) patterns enlarged in the software.

A great advantage of the system is that they can be sewn using the foot without the embroidery frame.

ENLARGING PATTERNS WITH OTHER SOFTWARE

Most of the programs that drive sewing machines include an option by which a line pattern can be enlarged. These will be different in each machine, so the following suggestions will need to be adapted to your sewing machine and software.

Choose the 'line' or 'shape' tool and the outline, shape or programmable fill option for stitches (depending on your program). Make sure that you have selected 'pattern', then draw a line (or narrow box shape) using the pattern option. Do not draw it the full length of the frame but only to about halfway. Now use the 'select' tool to grab a corner and pull it to make the design larger. If your software allows it, you could also try distorting it width-wise by pulling one of the handles halfway down, which often works better than just enlarging the whole thing. When you have a satisfactory line, copy and paste it to fill the frame, taking care not to go over the edges of the permitted stitch area. Fill your embroidery frame but do not try to go for matched straight lines. Instead, adopt a random approach of massed lines at different angles. When this is stitched, try stitching over earlier work in some areas, which could provide an interesting surface. Build in colour changes, especially when overstitching. If you are covering a large area, take the fabric from the frame, move to a new area of fabric, reframe and stitch again.

SPOT MOTIFS

A short line of pattern, drawn on the screen, will produce an individual motif, such as a

Fig. 10

A Bernina software screen showing single outline patterns that have been enlarged and used as spot motifs. The original size is also shown.

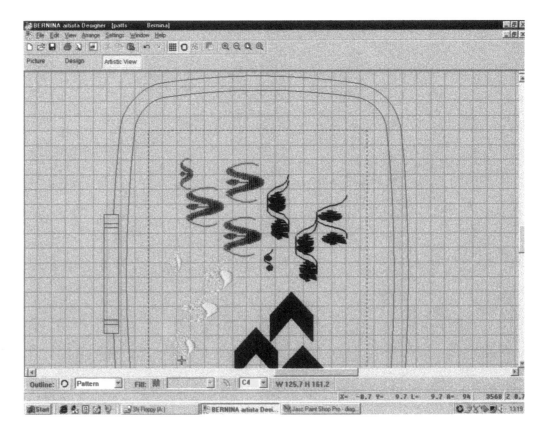

single scallop or flower (as opposed to a longer line, which would give a row of pattern). Selecting by copy and paste will allow a line to be built up of different motifs. These could be of different sizes. It is rather fiddly but can be saved and used for future projects.

CUT–AND–SEW FABRIC

The following method produces a fabric that can be used as a backing material or that can be cut out and applied to another background.

1   Cut 5cm (2in) squares from a variety of fabrics – sheer material, silks, cottons, velvets and so on – but give some thought to your colour scheme. You will also need a background cotton fabric in a toning colour.

2   Spray the background fabric with a low-tack adhesive, such as 505 spray, and lay the squares on the fabric in rows. Make sure that there is no more than one square of the same colour or texture in each row; check both horizontal and vertical rows for this.

3   Stitch the strips together with a three-step zigzag (stretch) stitch with a width of 6 or 7. Stitch in both directions, then cut each horizontal row between the stitching. Reverse each row of oblongs, checking that there are no matching oblongs in the new layout.

4   Still using the three-step zigzag stitch, sew the rows together, two at a time. Cut and sew the vertical rows again in just the same way. Repeat twice more.

At this stage, the piece can be used as it is or it can be cut diagonally, in one or both directions, with further stitching.

Fig. 11

In the cut-and-sew method squares of fabric are laid on a background and stitched. The fabric is then cut horizontally and vertically and alternate strips are reversed and restitched so that you end up with small squares. This is a useful method for blending diverse fabrics and colours.

Fig. 12

The fabric can also be cut diagonally to introduce tiny triangles to the pattern.

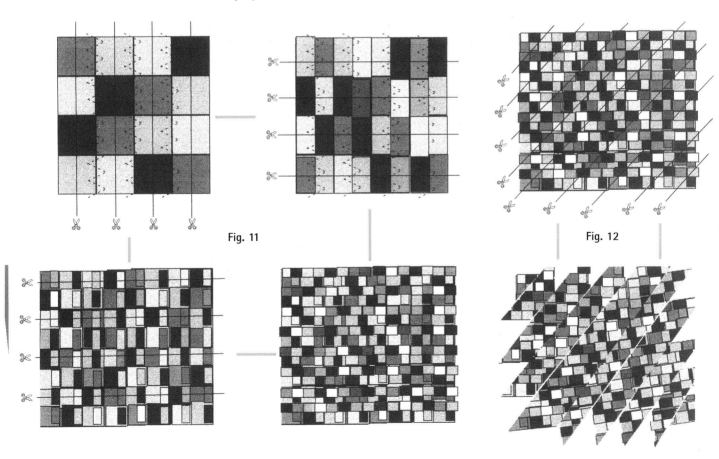

Fig. 11

Fig. 12

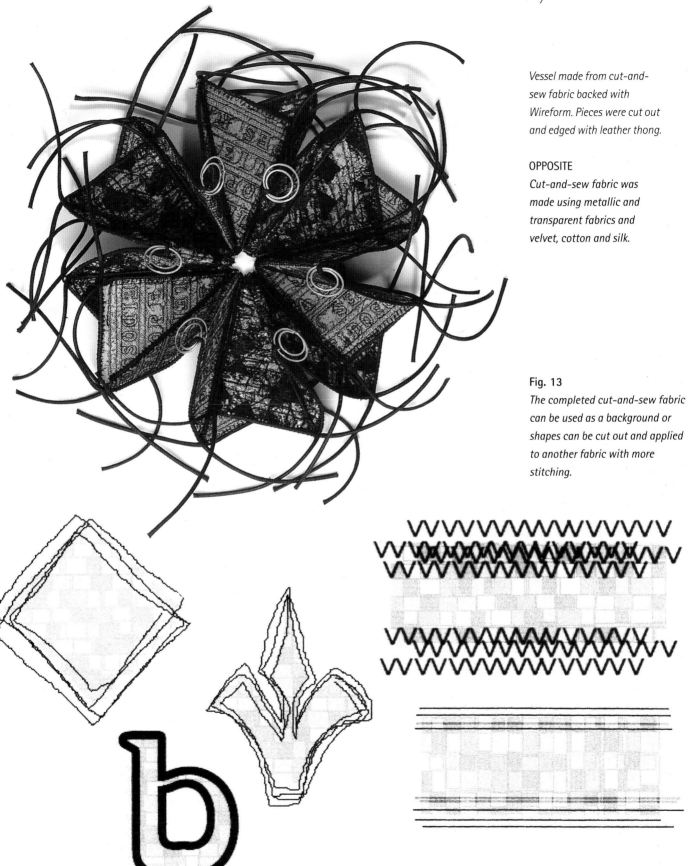

Vessel made from cut-and-sew fabric backed with Wireform. Pieces were cut out and edged with leather thong.

OPPOSITE
Cut-and-sew fabric was made using metallic and transparent fabrics and velvet, cotton and silk.

Fig. 13
The completed cut-and-sew fabric can be used as a background or shapes can be cut out and applied to another fabric with more stitching.

CRAZY PATCHED TEXT AND PATTERNS

This technique involves stitching text and/or patterns over a piece of felt, cutting it into irregular shapes and rearranging them before stitching them together again. The pattern will, of course, be an irregular mixture.

The stitching could be done on plain white felt with gold, white or cream-coloured thread and both fabric and stitching could be painted before being cut into shapes. Alternatively, use sepia-coloured thread or a shiny thread on coloured felt, using a thread that is a little lighter or darker in tone than the felt.

Stitch lines of pattern, such as letters or auto-pattern, around the edge of each shape, with a motif or larger pattern in the centre. If you intend to paint the fabric after stitching, do this now, using either silk or transfer paints. Then cut the fabric into irregular shapes and arrange these into a pleasing design, just like doing a jig-saw puzzle. Stitch the pieces together, edge to edge, using a three-step zigzag to prevent the material from cockling.

A book cover made using crazy-patched techniques on acrylic felt, stitched using automatic patterns and motifs from a Janome card. It was then treated with a heat tool and pieced together.

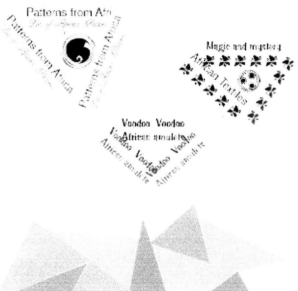

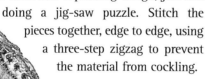

Layers of chevrons, stitched
chiffon and Xpandaprint were
treated with a heat gun. Cut-
out motifs were placed on top
and further stitching added.

Fig. 15
*Lines of patterns of different
sizes are worked on top of each
other, in the same direction or
in different directions, to build
up a richly patterned surface.
Chiffon can be added between
the layers and heat treated.*

OPPOSITE **Fig. 14**
*Lines of letters or patterns or a
combination of both can be
stitched in random triangles
over a piece of fabric and a
motif can be stitched in the
centre. The triangles are then
cut out and pieced together to
make a complete fabric.*

A small panel was made using automatic patterns in a grid structure, which was cut out and placed over a background fabric of velvet and chiffon. The background had been stitched using motifs digitized with the Brother PE Design software, treated with a heat tool and coloured with ChromaCoal pastels.

An alternative method would be to use an acrylic felt, many of which can be distressed by a heat gun. (Many ordinary felts react in this way, but whichever type of felt you choose, work on some samples before doing lots of stitching.) If you use Kunin felt, heat it after cutting it into pieces and before reassembly.

The edges could be burned or satin stitched depending on the overall design.

HEAT-TREATED FABRICS

Layers of stitched fabric can be built up and a heat gun used to burn or melt some of the top fabrics. Remember to wear a proper mask or respirator when you carry out techniques that involve burning. They are not expensive and will be a good investment. Lay some nappy (diaper) liner or stretchy, acrylic velvet over a base fabric of heavy calico or craft interfacing.

Stitch lines of built-in patterns, pinning and stretching the velvet as you work. Iron Bondaweb, which could be painted, over the top surface, and if you wish, lightly iron some metallic foil over this. Do not use too much. Now iron sheer fabric, such as chiffon, over the top, using a sheet of baking parchment to stop the iron from sticking. Use a heat gun to distress some of the top layers. Further layers of Bondaweb and chiffon can be added and distressed to give a crunchy, multi-layered surface.

CHANGING STITCH DENSITY TO ALTER THE TEXTURE

One way to change the look of the stitching is to alter the stitch density. This can be done quite simply by using a heavier thread or by winding a thread intended for hand-sewing on to the bobbin. Using two threads in the needle (see page 29) will give a similar

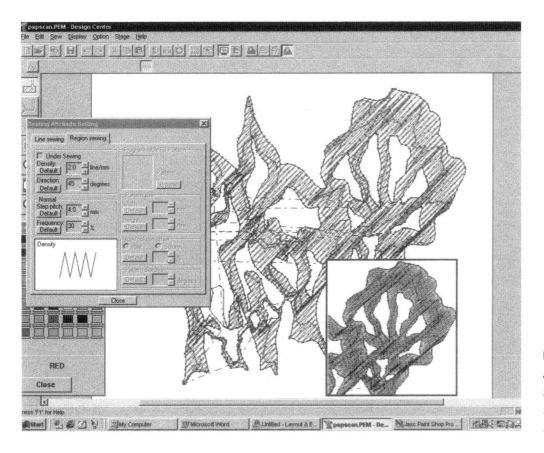

Fig. 16
A view of a screen using Brother software and showing the reduction in stitch density. The inset shows normal density.

effect, which can totally change the look of your stitching, whether it is free machining or automatic patterns.

Many modern sewing machines have an option that allows you to change the stitch density when using the embroidery unit. Reducing the density gives a much lighter effect, which can be useful for backgrounds. Experiment with this, starting with a low density and gradually increasing it.

Try some of the built-in motifs. They can look different with fewer stitches and can give an abstract, rather than a realistic, effect. Geometric motifs are suitable, especially if they are enlarged before the stitch

density is changed. The software for these machines often gives this option, and it can produce exciting results when it is used together with a change in the stitch angle.

This technique could be used for letters, grids, random long rectangles or even to echo any heavier motifs that are placed on top as patches. Think about the colour of the thread you use and how it affects both the background and anything going on the next layer. Finally, check the effects that can be achieved by using metallic threads on acrylic felt and then heating the background with a heat gun, or use this method instead of lines of pattern when you are working with heat-treated fabrics.

Chapter Two

Slips and Patches

4. Designing and Stitching

Slips are small motifs that are applied to a background after stitching. They have been used throughout history in many techniques, perhaps the best known examples being canvaswork and goldwork. We work in a similar way but refer to slips as 'patches'. In this part of the book we look at ways of creating a range of patches with a view to using them with the backgrounds that were discussed earlier.

There are many ways of making patches, ranging from free machine embroidery, large built-in patterns and motifs on cards, to using sewing machines with their own scanners and machines that link to a computer. Designs vary from simple shapes, used to form repeats or borders, to complex motifs derived from a variety of sources. The designs shown in Fig. 17, for example, are based on a study of painted fairground horses.

FREE MACHINE EMBROIDERY

Patches can be worked on all the fabrics described in this section and, although the filling techniques for them may vary slightly according to the fabric, the ideas suggested here will give a good variety of textures and patterns.

Several methods can be used to transfer designs to fabric, including:

- Holding the design and fabric to a light source (such as a window) and drawing over the lines.
- Using a light- or water-soluble pen to transfer the design lines.
- Drawing directly on to dark fabric with a gold pen or tailor's chalk.
- Making a stencil of the design and sponging paint through it.

Fig. 17
BELOW
Drawings from the decorated trappings of horses on a carousel.

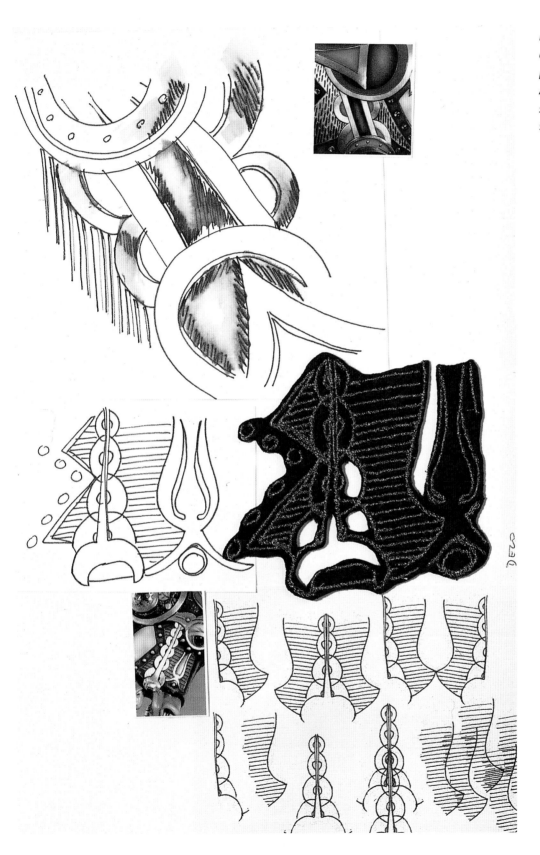

*Drawing of the trappings
on painted ponies, with the
patterns made from it.
A drawing was scanned and
stitched using the Janome
9000.*

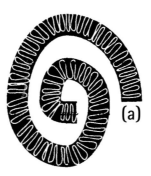

(a)

(b)

(c)

(d)

Fig. 18
A wide range of fillings for patches (slips) can be created with free running stitch or whip stitch. (a) Short lines across the pattern can be used, or the lines may run around the shape. (b) Alternatively, the shape can be filled with an open, circular scribbling, (c) with simple scribble or (d) with lumps and bumps created from irregular whip stitch.

LEFT A book cover was decorated with carnations embroidered with granite stitch and applied to fabrics that were made by stitching strips together and piecing them. The edges of the motifs were burned before they were stitched to the background.

Fig. 19

Normal tension (top) results in threads that lock between two pieces of fabric. Cable stitch (centre) has been worked with a loose top tension, with the thicker thread lying at the back of the work and the top thread wrapping it. Whip stitch (below) has been worked with a tight top tension; the loose bottom tension comes up to the surface and wraps around the top thread.

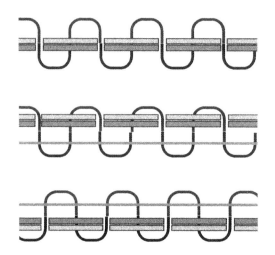

Adding patches is an exciting way of decorating pieces, especially when unusual fabrics and techniques are used. The fabrics can be decorated with free machining or by using embroidery machines. The treatment of the edges of the patches can also play a part in the design, and these are discussed in chapter 10, although the fabrics themselves generally dictate the most appropriate edging technique.

Transfer the pattern to your chosen fabric and place it in an embroidery ring. A simple spiral is shown in Fig. 18, and it can be filled with free running stitch, either across the width of the motif or following the outline. Work enough stitches to give the patch body when it is cut out. If you prefer, use granite stitch, forming tiny circles in layers so that they overlap each other and so that the shape of the circle disappears, leaving only a rough texture. This is particularly effective when it is worked with variegated metallic threads.

Another approach would be to fill the outline with free running stitch. Make 'blobs' at frequent intervals and build the stitching up in layers of different colours. You could fill the shape with random curved lines, making circles every so often and building up the

stitching in layers of different colours. The shape can be filled with whip stitch, either across the shape or following the contour. Vary the speed to give an irregular effect.

Alternatively, the outlines can be hand-stitched in a range of filling stitches, which could be used instead of, or in addition to, the machine stitching.

Altering the Tension

Good results can be achieved by altering the tension on the sewing machine to give additional texture or unusual effects, but this need not involve making drastic changes to the settings on your machine – for example, simply stitch some of the built-in patterns using a metallic thread on the bobbin and a plain rayon thread on the top. Look at the results on the bobbin side. Now stitch a few rows, first with a loosened top tension and then with a tightened top tension. Look at the results on the bobbin side. Repeat the exercise, but this time using a variegated thread. When the top tension is tightened and no stabilizer is used, lighter fabrics often pucker and distort in interesting ways. This can give results that resemble smocking and can look attractive if transfer fabric paints are ironed on to them after stitching. Experiment with a metallic thread on one of the many plain-coloured synthetic fabrics that are available. The result should be a textured and mottled colour scheme, with the stitching reflecting the colours with a subtle gleam.

Cable Stitch

Cable stitch can be used on patches, either by free machining or by using scanning and software techniques. Try winding a space-dyed hand-embroidery thread on the bobbin and working upside down. The thread should be thick enough to give a chunky, raised surface but should still pass through

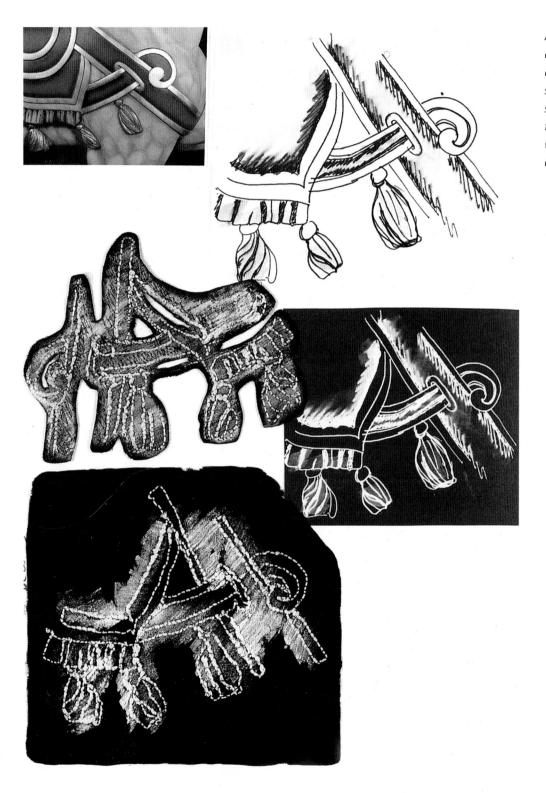

A sketchbook page with drawings of details of trappings on painted horses and the stitched pieces in cable stitching. One was worked with free machining, and the other was scanned into the Deco 600 and then stitched.

the bobbin tension without difficulty. Letters can be very effective stitched in this way, but remember that when they are worked upside down the motifs will be reversed. This does not matter if individual letters are being used as design elements, but it could be important if a word or entire phrase is to be read. Remember, too, to put the right side of the fabric underneath if you are using a stabilizer.

Whip Stitch

When you are working with whip stitch tighten the top tension as far as you can without the thread breaking. You should find that the bobbin thread will be pulled to the top of the work, wrapping itself over the top thread in the process. You may have to loosen the bobbin tension slightly by turning the screw on the bobbin case. If you do this, make sure that you know the position of the screw for normal sewing. Try winding several threads, in different colours, on the bobbin – you might have to wind the bobbin by hand – or use a slightly heavier thread. Experiment with a metallic thread on the bobbin and a variegated rayon thread on the top or use a monofilament on the top. Whip stitch looks particularly attractive when it is used in whirls, spirals or circles, and it can add a great deal of texture and interest to the motifs.

FABRICS FOR PATCHES

Having selected a motif and the method of stitching, it is time to think about the fabrics you will use. Most fabrics are suitable for patches, provided you consider the treatment of the edges before you begin. If you are using a fine fabric, such as silk, you will need to use a stabilizer of some kind, and this could be cut away close to the stitching to allow a more attractive treatment of the edges to be used. Some ideas for unusual fabrics are outlined below.

Water-soluble Fabric

Water-soluble fabric offers interesting opportunities for patches and can create unusual effects. You will have to stitch a grid first, using the foot or free machining, so that the stitches lock together, otherwise the fabric would wash away completely. For a looser, thicker line the grid could be stitched with a twin needle. Do this before you stitch the motif, and if you use one of the built-in patterns for this, the results can be very attractive.

After stitching the grid, draw the motif on the fabric and outline it in free running stitch (or use a scanned or a built-in motif), which should allow you to see it clearly. Now fill in the solid areas of the design with free machining. Use a design that has some open areas, because these will give a lacy effect. Any of the suggestions in Fig. 18 (page 45) would work well.

When the stitching is complete, trim the water-soluble fabric from around the patch, pin the motif securely to a piece of polystyrene or foam and hold it under running water until all the fabric has gone. Dab the piece with absorbent kitchen paper and leave it to dry thoroughly. Make several motifs in this way to apply to your chosen background.

Water-soluble fabric can also be used to stabilize fine fabrics such as chiffon, which could not be stitched on their own. Heavy stitching on chiffon can be interesting and the patch produced can be cut out and then frayed around the edges after the water-soluble fabric has been washed away. If you use chiffon you will not need to stitch a grid because the chiffon will provide the support.

Net

Stitching on net produces some surprising results. Heavy machine stitching can look very

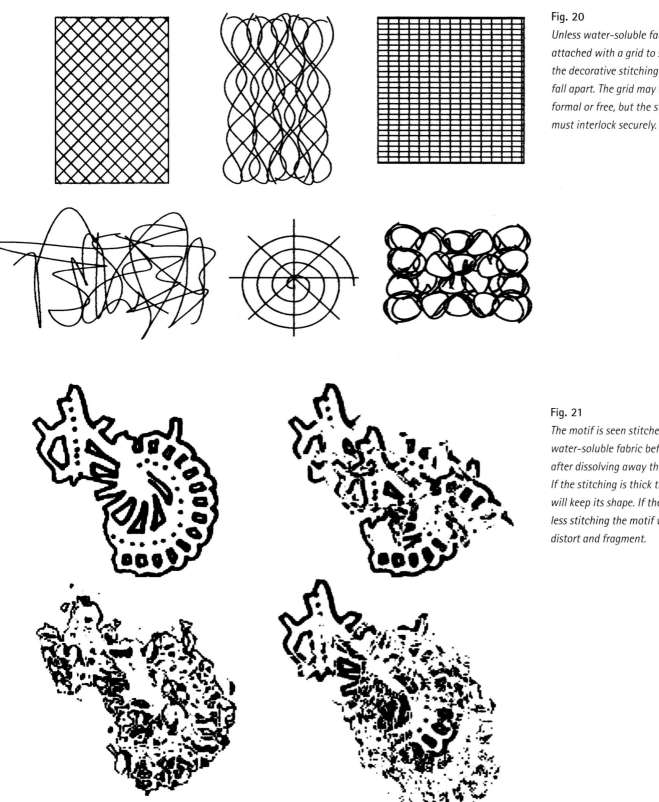

Fig. 20
Unless water-soluble fabric is attached with a grid to support the decorative stitching it could fall apart. The grid may be formal or free, but the stitching must interlock securely.

Fig. 21
The motif is seen stitched to water-soluble fabric before and after dissolving away the fabric. If the stitching is thick the motif will keep its shape. If there is less stitching the motif will distort and fragment.

Samples created with the Janome software and 9000 machine were stitched on water-soluble fabric using a design based on wrought iron gates. The water-soluble fabric was dissolved in cold water, and the piece was then ready to apply to a background.

effective, and because it can distort the net it is a particularly suitable material for small decorative bags and three-dimensional shapes.

Net can also be used to stitch patches. If the lettering facility on the machine is used to stitch large letters on two layers of net, the shapes will be subtly altered because the stitch will fall between different holes, giving an almost pixilated effect. The same effect can be achieved if you use a wide, close-set zigzag, which can be used for geometric effects. Draw a straight line pattern on the net with a marker pen and follow it,

foot down, feed dogs up. Check the result and make further samples. Border patterns could be made in the same way.

To add more body to the net, try the following process, which uses water-soluble paper:

1 Trap a piece of water-soluble paper between two layers of net.
2 Stitch lines of pattern and then cut the net into strips across the pattern lines.
3 Carefully dissolve the water-soluble paper, leaving much of it intact.

4   Leave the net to dry, then decorate it with paint; you could also add Xpandaprint or Markal oil stick.

5   Weave the strips together or through a grid.

An alternative method using water-soluble paper and net is to draw, print or computer-print your design on to the paper; you must use the special water-soluble paper that is sold specifically for the purpose. Frame two layers of net with the water-soluble paper on top. Stitch, leaving some areas free and making sure that the stitching is not too heavy.

When the stitching is complete, cut away any water-soluble paper that is not part of a motif. (Save it; it can be used again.) Now use nail varnish to mask areas of the design that you do not want to dissolve away, making sure that you follow cutwork rules so that areas are not isolated. When the varnish is dry, pin the piece to a support (see water-soluble fabric, page 48) and hold it under a cold tap. It will dissolve quickly, so make sure the water is a trickle, not a flood. Use a finger to nudge away unwanted paper. You can mould the pulp to some extent, too (see photograph on page 26).

These net bags were produced by stitching heavily on two layers of net, using either free machine zigzag stitch or a scanned design. The heavy stitching made the fabric malleable, and the bags can be manipulated into a variety of shapes.

Rows of automatic pattern were stitched on water-soluble paper, which was trapped between layers of net. Strips were cut out and partly dissolved, and Xpandaprint was added to give more texture. The strips were then woven through a metal grid that was completely covered with satin stitch worked with variegated thread.

RIGHT
A patch made from vanishing muslin and metal shim. The muslin was not completely washed away and was painted after stitching and teased out to give a distressed surface.

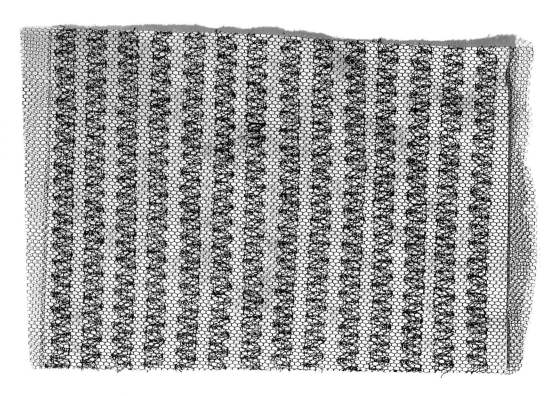

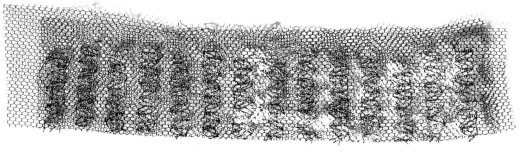

Dab the piece carefully with absorbent kitchen towel to remove excess moisture and leave it to dry overnight. The wet paper can be moulded or pinned at this stage and will dry in this shape. When it is completely dry, decorate it with paints or, if you prefer, use rubber stampers' ink and embossing powders. Use the embossing ink sparingly; sprinkle the powder over the design and use a heat gun until it bubbles. Metallic wax and Pearlex powders could also be used to gild the design.

Cut out the motifs close to the stitching and apply them to the background by hand or machine.

Vanishing Muslin

This fabric was widely used before alternative forms of water-soluble fabric become available. It is a support material, which can be removed after stitching by applying heat from an iron or a heat gun or by baking in the oven. Much the best way to use it, however, is to stitch and apply heat to parts of the design only, leaving behind a fragmented, frayed piece with an aged look. The effect is enhanced if the fabric is painted with silk paint beforehand.

To make a patch, stitch the design as usual before painting. The design can normally be traced directly on to the fabric, which is quite fine and can be held up to a window or placed on a light-box. When the design is stitched, apply heat with a heat gun or an iron. Use the point of the iron only on the areas you want to crumble away, leaving other areas intact. The crumbling can be helped if you tease the muslin gently with your fingers. Paint after crumbling, and remember that the thread will be coloured at the same time, which can add greatly to the effect. Metallic threads will resist paint.

A printed fabric with a flower design was backed with felt and stitched. This was cut into narrow strips, which were mixed up and spread out on a new backing. The three-dimensional flowers were scanned and stitched on felt using a Janome 9000.

An extension of this technique would be to hand-stitch some areas within the motif shape using a heavier thread and then to free machine over and around this. The contrast between the heavy stitching and the frayed, delicate areas works particularly well.

Felt

Felt is a particularly good fabric for patches because it can be cut close to the stitching without fraying. It is also a surprisingly pliable material and can be manipulated to hold its shape when heavily stitched, so that pieces can be wrapped around a pencil or kebab stick and will hold that shape. Any of the larger built-in patterns can be stitched on felt, cut out and used as patches. Alternatively, a closed zigzag stitch at the widest setting can be angled to give a line of chevrons, which can be cut out and used. Work hand-stitches into the patches or around the edges to give added emphasis. Some acrylic felts can be treated with a heat gun after stitching the patch. Wear a respirator when you do this. Further burning techniques could be performed with a soldering iron – for instance, the soldering iron could burn round holes or make marks, such as crosses.

Craft Interfacing

This type of interfacing is an excellent fabric for stitching patches because, like felt, it can be cut out close to the stitching. It can be painted before or after stitching, and transfer paints work particularly well on it.

Velvet

Motifs can be stitched on velvet very successfully. Interesting effects can be obtained because the stitching sinks into the pile, but if you prefer you can use water-soluble fabric to keep the stitches on top of the pile (see page 26). It can be difficult to deal with the edges on velvet, and these may be best handled by cutting around the motifs and then stitching into the background to secure them. The motifs could also be stretched over a small piece of mounting card and applied to a base fabric as a raised area.

Metal Shim

Fine metal shim can be machine embroidered to make motifs. It is available from specialist suppliers or, for a less expensive alternative, the inside of tomato or garlic purée tubes could be used. The metal can be free machined or patterns can be stitched with the foot in place. You might want to consider knocking back the shine when you use metal, and stitching is a good way of doing this.

Use a robust needle and keep it for metal work because it will become blunt with continued use. Always back with a heavy fabric, preferably the heaviest weight of interfacing, before stitching to stop jagged edges from breaking the thread. The thread itself makes a considerable difference because it colours the metal, and some of the darker variegated threads give a delightful effect.

The edges of the metal will be quite rough when the motif is cut out, and a good solution would be to cut roughly around the motif and then trim back the interfacing underneath so that just the metal is left at the edge. This can then be free machined to apply the patch to a background. It is possible to add both colour and texture to metal by the use of a transfer medium called Lazertran. Using a colour photocopier, an image (make sure you do not infringe copyright) can be copied on to the transfer medium, floated off in water and enamelled on the metal using a heat gun or in the oven (but not a microwave). This can add considerable

Machine embroidery was used to apply a patch made from fine metal shim to a background of computer-printed tissue paper, placed on heavy interfacing.

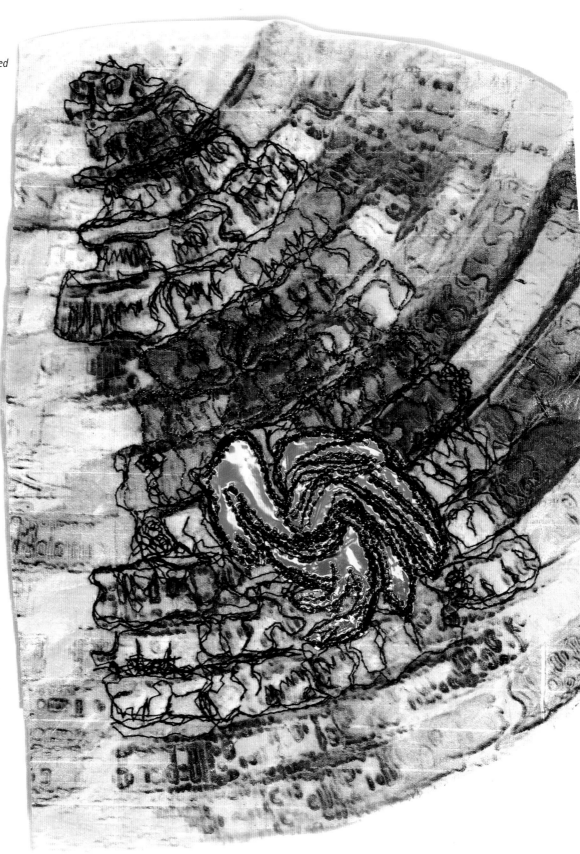

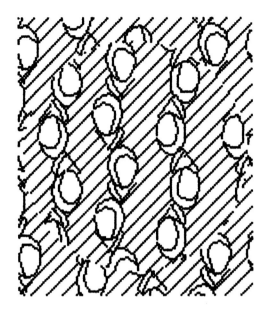

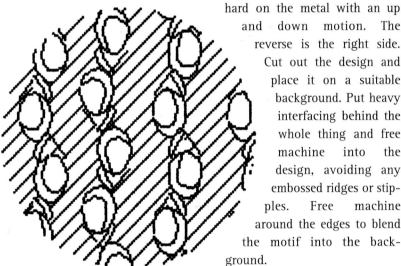

interest to the metal, but it is necessary to knock back the shine.

Metal shim (but not tomato purée tubes) can be coloured by being held in a gas flame. Hold brass or copper shim in a flame using tongs and an oven glove. Be careful not to hold it for too long – slow, careful heating produces the best results. Place the design for the patch over the metal and draw over the main lines using an old ballpoint pen (make sure there is no ink in it) or an embossing tool. The main lines should be etched lightly in the metal, then rest it on a magazine or mouse mat and press hard to emboss the design on the metal. Add detail by stippling – that is, dotting the pen hard on the metal with an up and down motion. The reverse is the right side. Cut out the design and place it on a suitable background. Put heavy interfacing behind the whole thing and free machine into the design, avoiding any embossed ridges or stipples. Free machine around the edges to blend the motif into the background.

USING DESIGNS FROM THE CARD

If you have a sewing machine with an embroidery unit you will already have some built-in designs or a card containing such designs. They could be digitized designs, which came with your software package, or you may have found the internet a rich source of such designs. Many of these designs are rather twee, but, with a little creative tweaking, they can prove to be a useful source of patches.

Fig. 22

The regularity of tatami stitch can be broken and made more interesting by overstitching with one of the built-in patterns.

A background of velvet, with applied nappy (diaper) liner, was decorated with patches digitized using the Brother PE Design software. Automatic patterns were then stitched over the entire surface in a Greek key design.

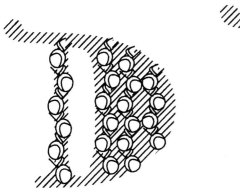

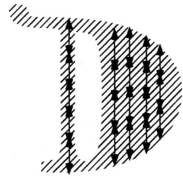

Fig. 23
Patches stitched with tatami stitch are overstitched with patterns that secure them to the background fabric.

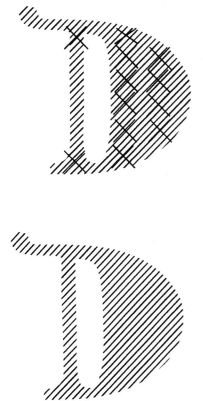

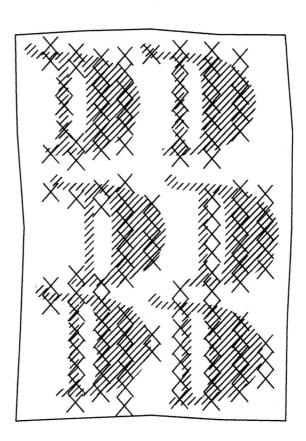

All of these can be stitched on unusual fabrics. Water-soluble fabrics and vanishing muslin offer exciting possibilities. Motifs stitched on felt could be cut out, burned away with a soldering iron or treated with a heat gun. Designs could be stitched in a self-colour on pale fabric, and then both stitching and background could be painted with silk or fabric paints. Using synthetic fabric and metallic thread with transfer paints will also give effective results. Overstitching designs or large letters with built-in patterns can create interesting effects. This works best where there are large areas of flat stitching and the pattern is used to break up the flat surface.

Samples for the cushion shown on page 96. These are the large quilting patterns supplied with the embroidery unit, and they were stitched in various sizes. Hand-worked running stitch was added afterwards.

Fig. 24
Hand-stitching can be added to a large machine-stitched star.

Hand-stitching into designs can add both colour and texture. Fig. 24 shows a quilting pattern that has been stitched in several sizes, with running stitch added to enhance the effect. This technique is most successful when it is used with the larger outline patterns, which can then be cut out to use as patches.

ALTERING PATTERN ELEMENTS

Many machines make it possible to miss stitches by including a facility to move on through the pattern, and this can be used to develop your design. Start stitching in the usual way and allow a defined area of the pattern to be completed. Then stop and move on, skipping an entire area or just a small part. This can work well with designs that lay down an outline stitch before filling, and a mix of outline and fill can be attractive.

Another way to use this facility is to stitch an entire motif in one colour and then to overstitch with a different colour, perhaps a

metallic thread, moving the machine on as described above.

Some machines have an option that allows part of the design to be isolated, generally by selecting one of the colours. Try the following:

- Stitch part of the image only. Some machines allow you to choose any segment while others make you start at the beginning each time.
- Change the colour during the stitching of a segment at a time when a colour change is not due.
- Stop after the understitching and move on.
- Create mirror images of part of the design.
- Rotate motifs.
- Move the image around the fabric or move the fabric in the frame.
- Work on the front and back of the fabric by removing it from the frame and turning it over.

Fig. 25
A pattern on a card can often be split into a number of elements, particularly at a colour change. The pattern can be moved on the sewing machine screen so that the individual elements make a more fragmented, less commercial-looking design.

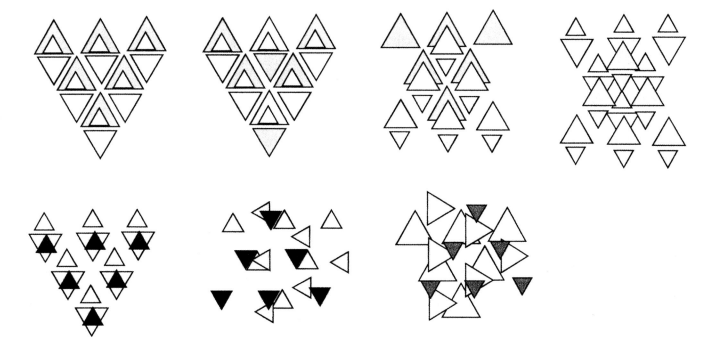

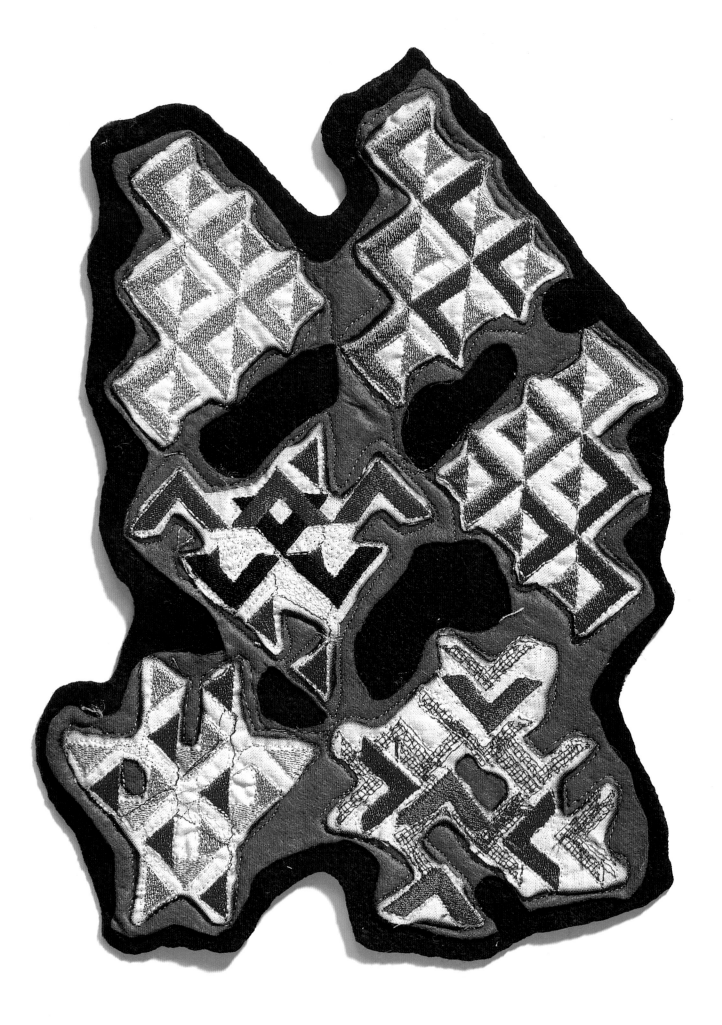

Fig. 26

A single pattern or part of a pattern on a card can be rotated or used as a mirror image at every repeat to build up quite complex designs. Extra stitching, using either the built-in patterns or free embroidery, can be added to integrate them with the background.

OPPOSITE

A design on a Pfaff embroidery card was partially worked, then rotated and moved and partially stitched again to break up the pattern's regularity.

FREE MACHINING INTO BUILT-IN DESIGNS

The use of free machining to outline motifs was described on page 46. The process can be taken a stage further by filling in areas of the design with free machine stitching.

Use an outline stitch – many of the individual designs have an outline as the final colour – and stitch this directly on the background fabric.

Opposite *The background was
decorated with rows of
automatic patterns worked
over strips of transparent fabric.
An outline of a rose from a
Janome embroidery card was
then stitched and laid on the
background, and the spaces
were filled in with granite
stitch.*

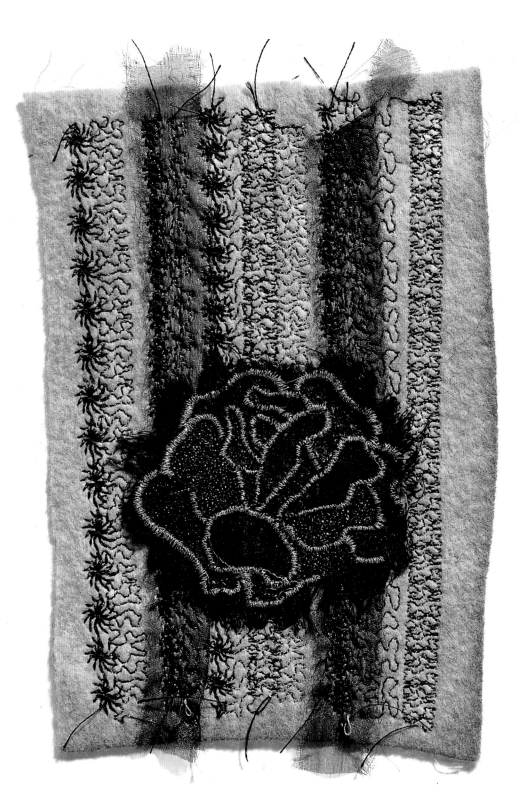

Set up the machine for free machining and
work some of the stitches described earlier
into the centre of the outlined area. Use a
contrasting colour or a metallic or a toning
thread.

5. Sewing Machine Scanners and Software

USING THE SCANNER

Some sewing machines offer the option of a scanning device. This is specific to that particular sewing machine and is not the same as a scanner used with a computer. Sewing machine scanners are hand-held and are used to 'read' a design and translate it to a card that the sewing machine can use. Although it is not vital to have a clear image for the sewing machine scanner, it is necessary to bear in mind that if the design is too complex it will give the scanner 'indigestion', although it will translate areas of texture as long as they are not too bitty. Some suitable designs are shown in Fig. 27. Use your own drawings or trace motifs from a book. Computer designs can also be used.

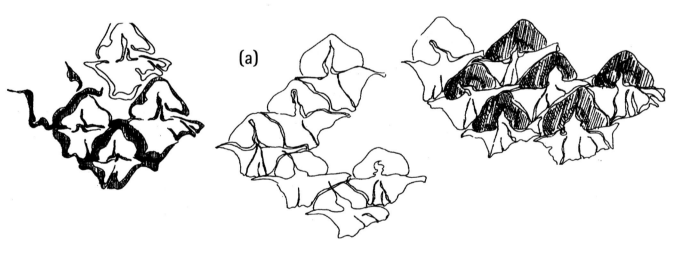

(a)

(b)

Fig. 27
*Drawings suitable for use
with a sewing machine scanner:
(a) combining thick and thin
lines and filled-in areas; a
pineapple skin.
(b) some cliffs drawn with a
felt-tipped pen.*

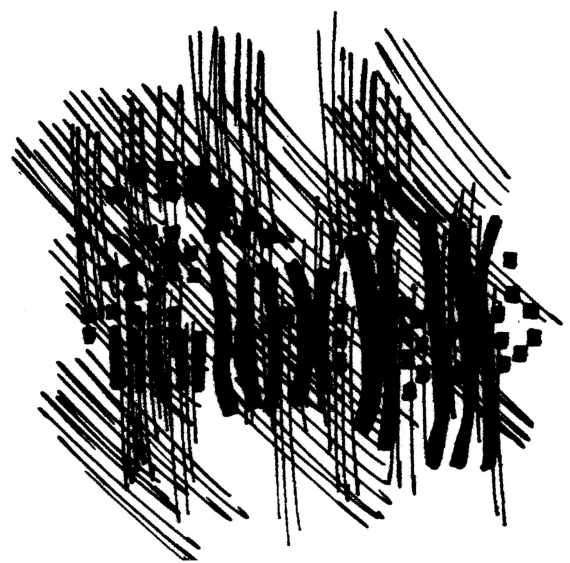

Fig. 28
*A drawing of a fabric through
a strong magnifying glass.
The solid pieces can be
scanned in with a sewing
machine scanner, and freely
stitched cross-hatching can
be added in a different colour
to attach them to the
background.*

OPPOSITE
*Outline shapes were
stitched on a background of
cut-and-sew fabric, using a
stylized tree motif (right)
previously scanned into the
Janome 9000 machine.
Filled shapes were then
applied using the same
motif. Emulsion paint was
added to part of the work.*

Designs can be stitched straight on to a
background, possibly one made using the
techniques described in Part 1. An alternative could be to stitch the scanned motif on
to fabric that has previously been stitched
by free machining or built-in patterns. It is
also possible to change the stitch settings
before scanning the motif. In addition to the
basic choice of an outline or filled motif,
there is often a further selection relating to
the angle of stitches. Some models offer a
cross-stitch option, which produces an

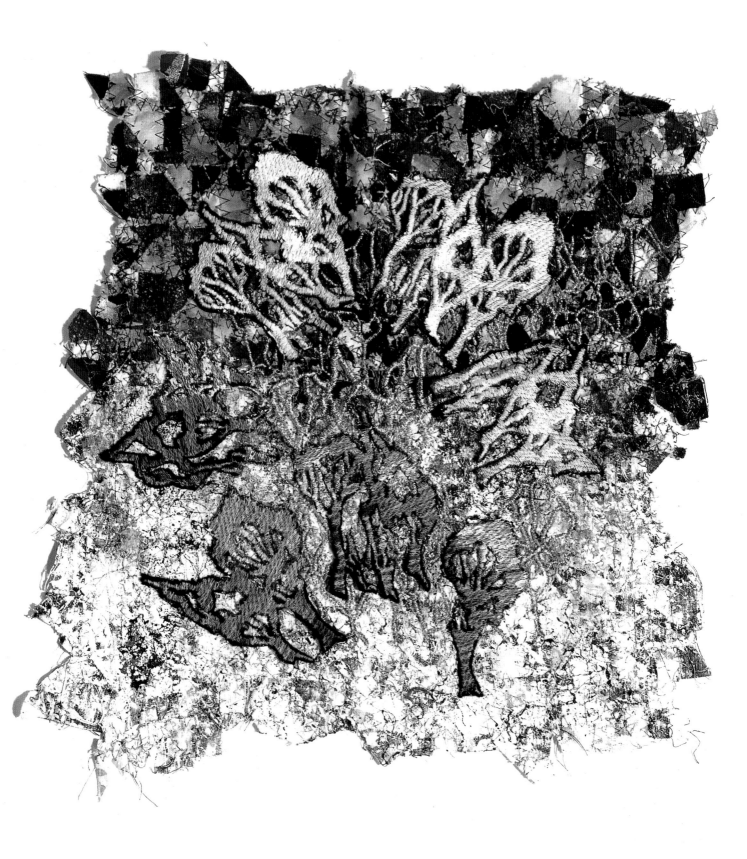

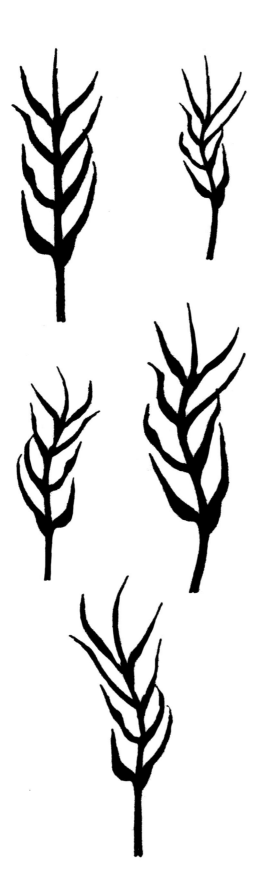

Fig. 29

A hand-scanner can scan in a straight line (the first leaf), or it can be wiggled around to give distorted shapes. These leaves were stitched and used in the piece illustrated opposite.

effect similar to small mosaic squares on the bobbin side of the work, and the use of a metallic thread on the bobbin will enhance this effect.

There is no need to change the design for filled or outline motifs. If a solid design is scanned in on the outline option, only the outlines of that design will be stitched. With the fill option, however, what you see is what you get, and the solid areas will appear just as they are drawn.

Distorting the Scan

When you use a scanner it should be drawn smoothly and steadily across the design. However, if you try pulling the scanner towards you and then away from you, still working smoothly, the design will become mirrored and interesting shapes will emerge. Strip scanning involves drawing the scanner over the source for about 2.5cm (1in), then lifting it and moving it, at an angle, to another area and repeating the scan. You can continue to do this until the design area is full. The technique does call for a steady hand, however, and some practice will be needed.

Another good way of distorting the scan is to take a fairly solid design and dab around the edge with typing correction fluid. This gives a wonderfully distorted edge, with areas of textured stitching. Take the process a step further, and other areas of the design can be 'splattered' to give a different effect. Look at the bobbin side of the work.

Overstitching

Large areas of pattern can look rather flat and dull. Consider stitching over them with built-in patterns. Using a thread in a contrasting colour will produce some exciting effects.

Strips of transfer-painted papers and fabrics were woven together, and skeletonized leaves were laid on top. Black chiffon was laid over the whole piece, and free machining was used to emphasize the leaf shapes. The leaves around the edge were worked on the Janome 9000 using a scanned drawing that was distorted during scanning (see diagram 29).

Textured Effects

Using different threads at the top and bottom or heavier threads on the bobbin, as described under cable stitch (see page 46), can make an enormous difference when you are stitching scanned designs. The bobbin side of the work can often be the more attractive, especially when designs contain such elements as small circles or linear elements that have been scanned in satin stitch outline mode. Think 'mark-making' when you are designing. Use a black pen and produce a sampler showing the effects of different marks and shapes, paying particular attention to the bobbin side of the work.

Layered Scans

Think about stitching scans over scans. You could, for example, scan the same design as both outline and filled stitching. Stitch the outline design all over the fabric first and then stitch the heavier one over the top. Alternatively, try the process the other way round, with the outline breaking up the heavier scan, which was stitched first. Try

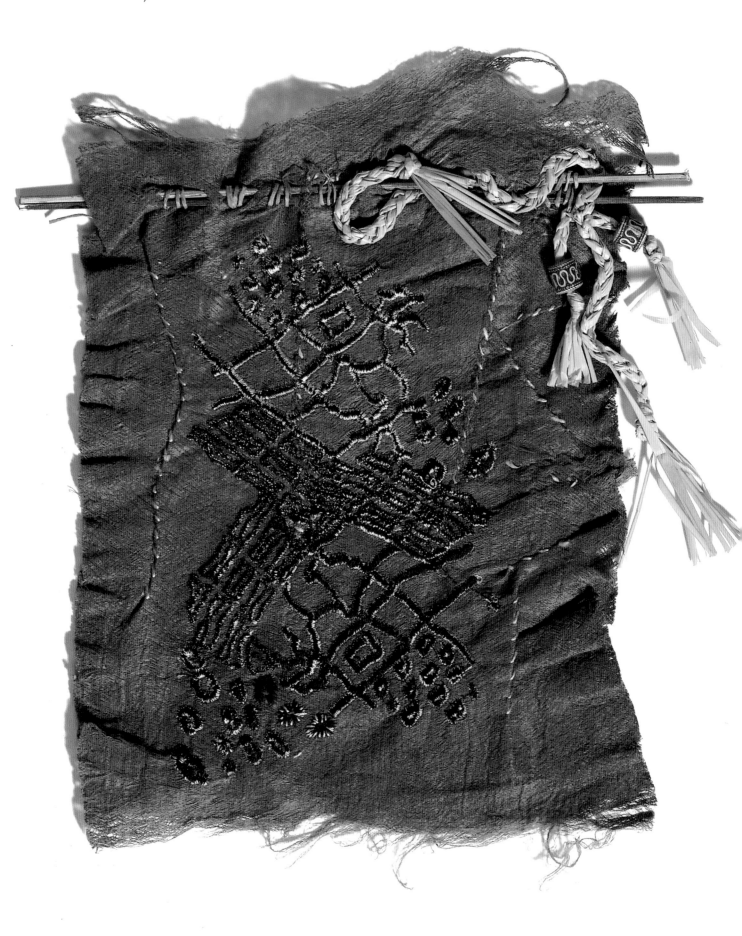

stitching a filled scan, with another, slightly offset, on top. This approach can produce interesting shapes, so do not be afraid to experiment. Use all the fabrics and techniques suggested earlier in this section, but stitch them using the scanned image and the embroidery unit.

You could also try stitching another motif exactly over the top of the previous one using the registration marks; this will be described in the manual for your particular machine. For example, you could trace the negative shapes in the background of the design and stitch as filled stitching. Trace again, using the main areas of the motif, also filled with stitching, but in another colour. Tracing a third time could give the outline of the design, worked using an outline stitch.

USING SEWING MACHINE SOFTWARE

Many modern sewing machines have software that makes it possible for designs to be scanned into a computer and used to produce patches that are then stitched on the sewing machine. This differs from a machine's scanner in that it offers more

Fig. 30

Scans can give linear or filled results. This leaf was scanned three times and each was stitched on top of the other. First, the background shapes were scanned using the tatami filling stitch. Then the solid leaf shapes were scanned, also using tatami stitch but worked with a different colour thread. Finally, the third scan was done using a narrow satin stitch and worked in a third colour.

A scanned image (left) and digitized image (right) demonstrate that there is little to choose between these methods for creating simple shapes.

OPPOSITE
Mbuti designs were the inspiration for the pattern, which was worked in simple stitching. Bark cloth was used as the background, and the stitching was worked with black thread on the bobbin and a variegated thread on the top. The tension was adjusted so that the top thread was visible underneath. The work was designed to be viewed from the bobbin side.

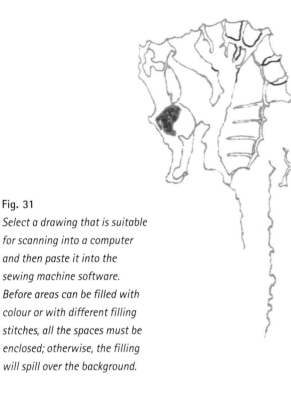

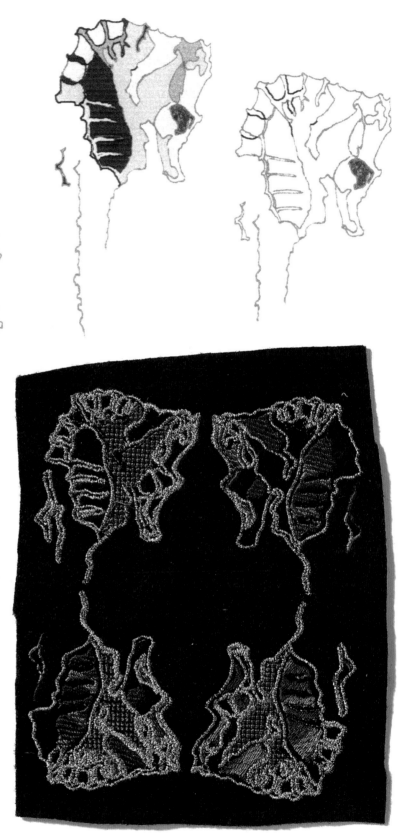

Fig. 31

Select a drawing that is suitable for scanning into a computer and then paste it into the sewing machine software. Before areas can be filled with colour or with different filling stitches, all the spaces must be enclosed; otherwise, the filling will spill over the background.

The drawing shown in Fig. 31 was digitized using the Bernina Artista software and stitched on felt using a mixture of rayon and metallic threads.

OPPOSITE **Fig. 32**

These are just some of the filling patterns that are used by sewing machine software. They will, of course, vary from program to program.

control over the stitching and its placement. With some systems, the difference is not marked, but in others the effects could be completely different. The process of converting from an original image to a stitchable motif is known as digitizing a design. Some of the programs are extremely sophisticated, and it is possible to produce a wide variety of patterns and textures using the options provided. Lettering can be a good design source, and all the software packages have a good selection of fonts and a range of built-in devices to vary and enhance the placement of text. Letters can also be used as design elements, and in addition to the more usual monograms that are available, individual letters can be flipped, rotated and made into mirror images or built into borders. When the designs are complete, they can be transferred to the sewing machine via a cable or reader/writer box.

Your own drawings can also be scanned directly into the machine's program. The success of the process will often depend on the length of time you spend getting the drawing right. Unlike the scanning option, texture does not translate well, and it is better to add this later. Aim to produce a clear drawing with all the lines sharp and no gaps where one line joins another. Fig. 31 illustrates the type of drawing that is needed.

There are many ways to fill the drawing with stitching, but most work on the 'paint bucket' type of program, which require a closed area of one colour, otherwise it will leak. All the programs offer fill and outline stitches, and many have a range of patterns that can be used for both purposes. Fill stitches include satin stitch, which is good for small areas, and a form of tatami or fill stitch, which is more practical for large areas of stitching. Outlines are usually single or triple, which is good for quilting, satin stitch or patterns, which are similar to the built-in patterns on the machine.

By themselves the patterns are often regular and can look too perfect, so they are better broken up and used in small areas. To create

The motif was digitized using the cross stitch fill available in the Janome software. This is the bobbin side of the work, which gives a delightful mosaic-like appearance. It is based on drawings from wall paintings.

some interesting textures for filling stitch begin by breaking up a large space into several smaller ones. Fill the main area with tatami or step stitch and the smaller areas with a pattern or even two different patterns. This will break up the main pattern area, while giving an intriguing glimpse of patterns that come and go. Experiment to see which patterns work best for this method. It is especially effective when the stitching is worked in metallic thread.

Try stitching narrow bands of pattern worked in grids, both formal and informal.

Broken grids giving areas of pattern can be used with more flowing designs providing a contrast. The use of pattern fillings plays an important part in all these ideas.

Outlining designs can tidy them up and make them look finished. A narrow satin stitch is better than a heavy one, which can look clumsy, and all machines have options for change the size of the stitch.

When you are working on water-soluble fabric you can use the outline stitches to form a grid on which the motifs are stitched. Lay down a grid of outline pattern stitches and then digitize a motif separately, copying and pasting it on top of the grid. When the design is transferred to the sewing machine, the machine will stitch the grid first and then place the motif on top. If you use water-soluble fabric with the embroidery unit you will have to use a heavier fabric (or use two thicknesses of the medium-weight fabric).

Understitching

Use the understitch facility on your machine for designs that have areas of heavy stitching. This lays down widely spaced zigzag stitches under the motif and avoids stretching and distortion, although, of course, distortion can sometimes be attractive and be made into a feature of the work, allowing ripples and movement to flow through it. The understitching can vary in density, and this should be set and the 'option' box for understitching checked before the designing begins.

Stitch Density

The software on your machine may include an option that allows the density of the stitches to be changed. Stitching the same motif or letters in different densities can give a textural result, and this is a good method of turning built-in designs into abstract ones.

Experiment with the different stitch densities available on your machine. Try the same motif several times, using a different density each time and observe the difference. The illustration on page 77 shows this effect.

Overstitched Designs

Motifs can be stitched over motifs without your having to move the frame, and this often allows the colour below to show through, especially when a metallic thread has been used, either underneath or over the top. Changing the density of the stitch is an attractive option in these circumstances, and combining different fill patterns can give attractive results. For example, you could design a motif using a solid fill stitch to be worked in a plain thread. Copy the motif and, on the copy, change the colour and alter the density and pattern so that far fewer stitches are used. Paste this over the original motif. When it is stitched, the machine will automatically stitch the second, less dense, motif over the first.

Colour

It is tempting to think that because you control the thread colour physically at the stitching stage, there is no need to bother with it at the digitizing stage. You do, however, need to build in some colour changes, even if you are planning a one-colour design. The purpose of this is to give a 'back-stop' when stitching; it is much easier to return to a colour halfway through a

Fig. 33

When you use filling patterns you can choose different densities to give the stitching more depth.

Fig. 34

A view of the screen showing a design element that has been copied and pasted. The pasted image is altered by using the density control and then placed back over the original.

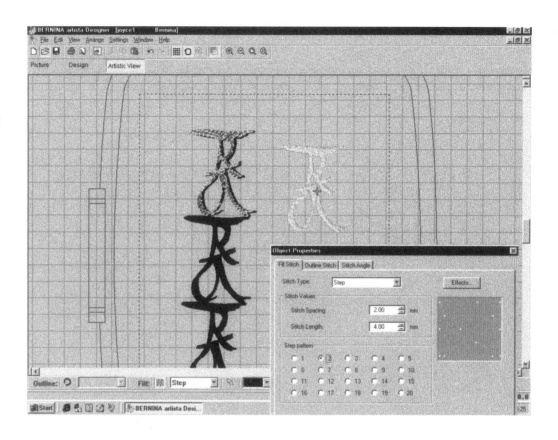

Fig. 35

Colour change is shown with Janome software. The inset shows the original scan.

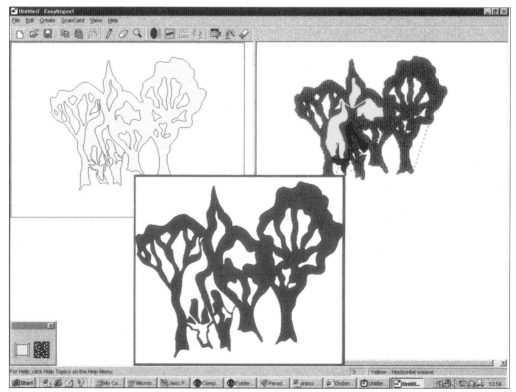

complex design if the stitching goes wrong, even if the thread is not changed.

When you are copying and pasting a multi-coloured motif, it is useful to check the menu option that controls colour order before you finish digitizing. This allows the stitching of one colour to be fully completed before the second colour is started, and so on. Otherwise, you may find yourself using all the colours for each motif, with all the re-threading that would entail.

TEXTURE

Patches produced using the digitizing process sometimes look rather flat. Ideas for avoiding this are included in Part 3, but you can use outline patterns at the digitizing stage. Try outlining a complex shape and, if you have chosen the right pattern, the stitches will twirl into strange shapes and climb up each other to form ridges. The end

result may not look much like the original shape, but it might be more interesting.

Large, flat areas of fill stitching could be over-stitched using outline patterns to break up a large area; see Figs. 22 and 23 on pages 57 and 59.

Texture can also be added by altering the sewing machine tension as you stitch, although some machines take control of the tension when stitching automatically and do not allow you to change it during the stitching process.

Finally, remember that all the fabrics discussed earlier – water-soluble fabric, net, vanishing muslin and so on – can be used with motifs that are generated by the design software. Just take care when you place the fabric in the frame and use water-soluble fabric as a stabilizer if necessary.

Lettering was stitched using the Artista software for the Bernina 180. The density was changed to alter the look of the text. The picture on the left shows letters stitched using a heavier thread on the bobbin.

6. Cutting out the Patch

The final step in preparing a patch is to consider the methods by which the shape can be isolated before it can be applied to the chosen background – it could be cut out with scissors, torn or burned away from the background fabric.

The fabric that was used for stitching the patch will, generally, dictate the way that it will be treated. If water-soluble fabric was used, for example, it could be dissolved away after stitching. Alternatively, the edges could be frayed, turned under and hemmed or stitched to the background.

If a patch is machine embroidered on two layers of polycotton fabric with metallic

threads on both the spool and the bobbin it is possible to burn it away from the backing fabric with a soldering iron. The metallic threads are more resistant to burning than rayon ones. Polycotton is a good background fabric because it is not as smooth as synthetic fabrics and it burns well, being less resistant than cotton to burning. When you are designing a patch for this technique, bear in mind that the negative shapes should not be too large or they will flop about, out of the design, but nor should they be so small that is becomes impossible to get the soldering iron into them. Some solid areas will help to add rigidity to the patch. The design shown on page 80 was based on distorted lettering. It was stitched in satin stitch with the foot

Samples worked for the vessel shown opposite use a drawing scanned into, and stitched on, the Deco 600.

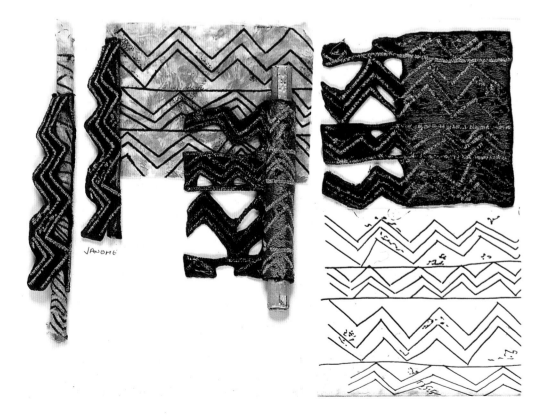

A vessel worked using the samples shown in the photograph opposite, which were rolled around large paper beads made from printed computer designs of the same chevron pattern and secured to each other with zigzag cord.

The samples shown here were burned with a soldering iron and stitched together. This gives sufficient rigidity to form a small container.

Vessel made from the samples above. The lettering was distorted in a computer paint program and stitched using free-machine techniques. Polycotton was used as the background fabric, and metallic thread was used on the bobbin as well as on top of the machine.

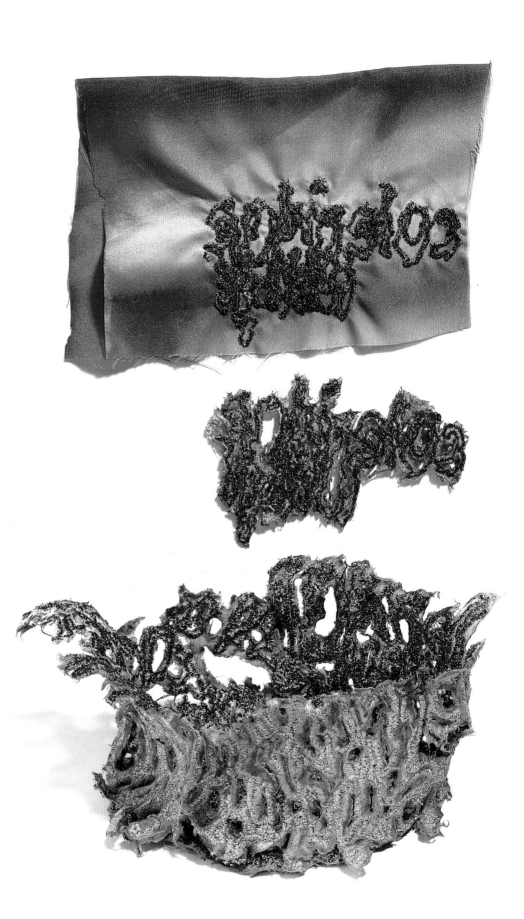

down and feed dogs up, and the fabric was pulled to follow the shape of the letters as they were stitched. Some areas were made more solid with machine embroidery.

When the shapes have been stitched, leave them in the embroidery frame and use a hot soldering iron to burn away the fabric inside the shape. Wear a mask or respirator and always hold and use the tool so that it points away from your body. Take care that you do not burn your fingers. You might find it helpful to place the frame on an old metal tray or other heatproof surface. When the inside areas are done, work around the edge of the shape.

The burned-away patch should be quite rigid and should hold its shape well. It can be decorated with silk paints or runny fabric paints; remember that metallic threads will resist the paint. When several motifs have been made in this way, they can be applied to a background made using any of the methods described in Part 1. They could also be joined to make a container of some kind.

This method of burning patches adds a rigidity and an attractive edge to the patch. Fabrics other than polycotton could be used and will give very different results. Sheer fabric, for example, will burn very easily.

Layers of sheer fabric in different colours could be stitched together, and a soldering iron with a very fine tip could be used to burn through the top layers to reveal the colours below.

Acrylic felt also gives good results, and a soldering iron could be used as a tool for making marks. Push it into the felt to make round holes or draw it in diagonal lines or crosses.

Take care with all these burning techniques that you do not isolate an area, because it will fall out. The old rules of joins and bridges that apply to cutwork also apply here.

The edges could also be hand-stitched, with an edging stitch such as buttonhole. Alternatively, they could be cut out of a 'frayable' fabric and the edges pulled to give a distressed appearance – take care that you do not pull away the stitching. Cut edges could be hemmed or left as they are, ready for you to free machine them and merge them into the background fabric.

At the end, when the patches have been cut or burned away, you will find yourself with pieces of leftover fabric. Trim the fabric leftovers and piece them together to make a new background as shown in Fig. 36.

Fig. 36
When you cut stitched patches out of the fabric you are left with lots of spare pieces. Rather than throw them away, piece them together to make another background.

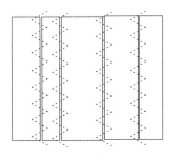

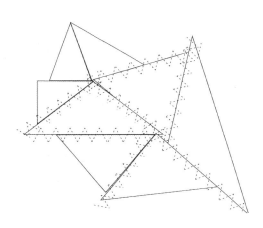

Chapter Three

Putting it all Together

7. Applying Motifs to the Background

Now that you have produced a background and have some patches (slips) to place on it, you can begin to think about the best ways to secure the patches and the various layers together. Obviously, it is important to make sure that the different elements are firmly fixed together, but there are many ways in which this can be done that will also enhance the appearance of the work. Always consider the overall effect of the piece. If the motifs are strong, for example, they may not need any extra stitching, in which case securing them to the background will be all that is needed.

Give some thought, too, to the overall shape of the piece. If it is a wall-hanging or panel, should it be rectangular, cruciform or an irregular shape? Will it be in one piece or made up from several pieces? Will it be framed or free

Bands of pattern on baked felt were placed on a background of velvet, with nappy (diaper) liner on top, and then the piece was heavily stitched with automatic patterns and couched ribbons.

The box was made from squares that were scanned and stitched on the Deco 500 and applied to velvet, which was completely covered with automatic patterns stitched on the Pfaff 7550.
(Lynn Horniblow)

hanging? If it is going to be hung up, think about the hanging mechanism.

The positioning of the motifs is, of course, crucial to the success of the work, but at this stage you should also consider bands and borders. Does the work need a border? If so, where and how should it be placed – all around the edge, at the top and bottom only or down the sides only?

ARRANGING THE MOTIFS

One advantage of working with cut-out motifs is that they can easily be rearranged on the background so that you can achieve the most pleasing design. Keep in mind the following points:

- Use an odd number of motifs: 3, 5 or 7 will look better than 2, 4 or 6.
- Consider the negative shapes – that is, those that are formed between the patches.
- Do not make the work too busy by applying too many motifs.

Bands of pattern can be applied to the background or worked directly on to it. The bands can enhance the motifs by emphasizing their position, or they can be used to form a grid with the patches placed within it. Borders can be made in the same way and used to define the edges or to divide the background into different areas or shapes.

When you are putting all the elements together, the initial design could be made by using collage techniques. You could tear printed images from magazines, for example, choosing colours and textures that roughly match the background fabric. You could also tear or cut out images in the shape of the stitched elements, again choosing colours and textures that correspond to the colours and shapes of the stitching.

If you have access to a computer and a design package both the patches and the background could be scanned so that you can experiment with the positioning of the motifs. Computers make light of 'what if?' operations and allow many options to be explored comparatively quickly.

STITCHING

When the design has progressed to the stage of a working drawing and you are happy with the positions of the pieces, it is time to think about the techniques that can be used to bring the work together.

Outlining with Stitch

Pin the motifs in position and free machine all around them, covering the edges with multiple rows of stitching. Depending on the effect you want to achieve, you could stitch just one or two lines or use very heavy stitching, which will blend with the background.

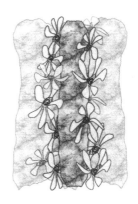
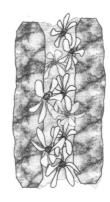

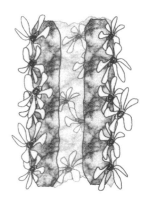

Fig. 37

Each of these diagrams shows a different placing of flower patches on an embroidered background. These embroideries could be small wall panels, doubled to make book covers, rolled round to make cuffs or, if made in delicate fabrics, used as sections of a lampshade.

If you want a quilted effect you could place the background material on wadding with a calico backing and then machine around the motifs to raise them. Whether you use wadding or not, an interesting effect can be obtained by working further lines of stitching to radiate away from the motifs.

The outline stitching could be done with a matching thread or in a contrasting colour. Using whip stitch or couched thread could provide a textural contrast in the outline stitching, and putting a thicker thread on the bobbin and working upside down, following the previously stitched outline, would add texture and also offer an opportunity to use an attractive space-dyed thread.

ALL-OVER STITCHING

Placing the motifs on the background with lines of stitching over the top will have the effect of uniting the patches with the background. The weight of the stitching is vital here: lines of straight stitch worked up and down the piece will give a lighter effect than thicker, built-in patterns, but the latter could look wonderful if they were used over a patch that was made up of large areas of flat stitching. The patterns will add interest to the motif and, at the same time, help to merge it into the background. This could be carried a stage further if you used a thicker thread on the bobbin for cable stitch.

Some ideas for all-over stitching are shown in Fig. 38. They include the use of lettering stitched in straight lines over the patch, scribbling with free machine stitching, working granite stitch around and over the motif and using blocks of satin stitch over the motif and background. Straight lines of stitch could also be used to enclose the

Fig. 38

There are many ways of attaching patches to a background. You can stitch all over them, using patterns or with free embroidery, or you can stitch around the edge of each patch with free running stitch, whip stitch or cable stitch.

A detail of a panel showing some motifs stitched directly on the background and others stitched on vanishing muslin or burned polycotton, which was applied on top.

OPPOSITE
A panel with digitized stitching on silk in the central area and borders made from the same design but stitched on polycotton and burned.

motif, and these could radiate out into the background. It is also possible to stitch curved lines – some satin stitch, some running stitch – over the motif, following any lines in the composition of the patch.

It is even possible to stitch so densely that the motifs become part of the background, allowing you to apply further patches on top. These could be variations of the background motifs but with a change of scale to add interest.

LAYERING PATCHES
Combining background stitching with bands of pattern or cut-out shapes can give exciting results.

1   Work some motifs directly on to the background fabric. Using a technique such as applying nappy (diaper) liners

to velvet or heat-treating fabric would allow these to sink a little into the background.
2   Stitch the same motif as the patch on a material such as felt. Change the size of the motif to enhance it and make use of the alteration in scale. Make several patches.
3   Apply the patches to the background, placing them directly over the top of the previously stitched motifs or using them as a group placed elsewhere.

USING THE SAME DESIGN
Working the design on the main body of the piece and using patches as borders can also create interesting effects. Use a different technique for the edging patches – for example, stitch them in a plain colour in the main area and burn them away with a soldering iron for the borders.

'Synchronized Swimmers' by Natalie Cone. This detail, from a large panel, shows motifs that were applied to heavy background stitching worked using free machine techniques. The heads and feet of the swimmers are shown above the water and are loosely attached rather than stitched down to the surface.

Fig. 39

Patches can be joined together by pinning them to water-soluble fabric and then completely covering the whole area with a twin-needle grid. When the fabric dissolves the stitching is looser and more textured than if it had been stitched with a single thread.

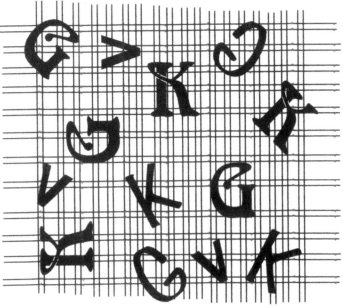

CUTTING UP PATCHES

Do not despair if you have a disaster – the motifs might look too heavy when they are placed on the background, for example, or the design might look unbalanced so that the overall piece does not work. Try cutting up the worked patches so that you can rearrange them, but look at the shapes carefully before you cut them up and move them. The repositioned patches will have to be stitched firmly in place, and you will need to stitch the cut areas securely into the background, particularly if the cut edges have loose stitching that must be fastened down. This will produce a new, highly textured background to which you can add some new patches.

PARTLY ATTACHED PATCHES

It will not always be necessary – or desirable – to stitch down the motifs around the entire outline. It may be sufficient to stitch part of the motif to give the work a three-dimensional element. In the hanging shown on the left-hand side, the figures are worked as patches and attached to the fabric in such a way that their upper bodies and feet appear to be above the water, making them look like swimmers. The acanthus leaves illustrated on page 2 were treated in the same way. To do this, simply stitch, by hand or machine, the area of the patch that needs to be fixed to the base. Make sure that the stitching is secure and that the loose piece does not flop but is firmly raised above the background.

WATER-SOLUBLE FABRIC

Previously stitched patches could be attached by placing them on water-soluble fabric, with free machine stitches going over the edge of the patches and continuing on to the water-soluble fabric. Further patches could be applied in this way. It is important that the patches themselves should not be too heavy, or the composition will be unbalanced.

1   Lay out the motifs on a sheet of water-soluble fabric. Assess the design and pin all the patches on the water-soluble fabric in an attractive way, bearing in mind the negative spaces.
2   With the machine set for free running stitch, work over the edges of each patch and into the water-soluble fabric. Make sure that all the stitches on the water-soluble fabric have further stitches worked over them to lock them together; if you do not do this they will unravel when the fabric is dissolved.
3   When the stitching is complete, pin the work to a firm, waterproof background, such as a polystyrene tile. Trickle water over it to dissolve the fabric, continuing until all the stickiness has gone from the joined areas. Leave to dry on the tile so that the piece keeps its shape.

Fig. 40
To join patches with water-soluble fabric or paper, pin each patch to the fabric, which is held in a frame, and work free running stitches across the spaces between the patches.

Large letters were scanned and stitched into the Janome 9000, cut out and laid on water-soluble fabric. The whole piece was then stitched with a twin needle, and the water-soluble fabric was dissolved. The embroidery was laid on a piece of felt, decorated with Xpandaprint and stitched again.

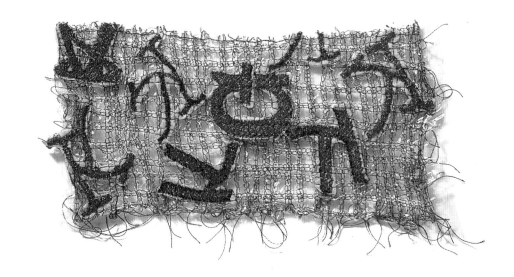

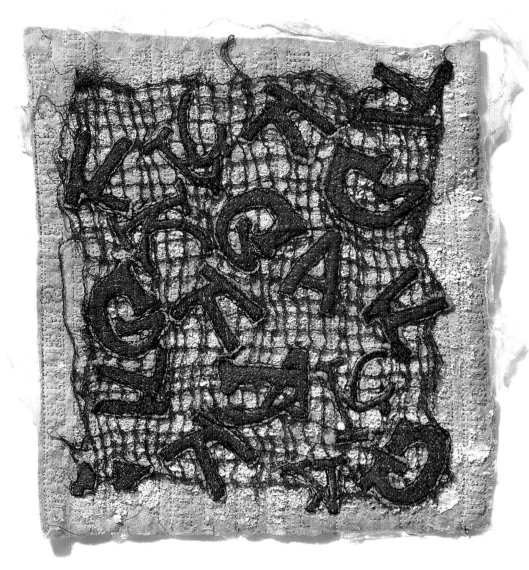

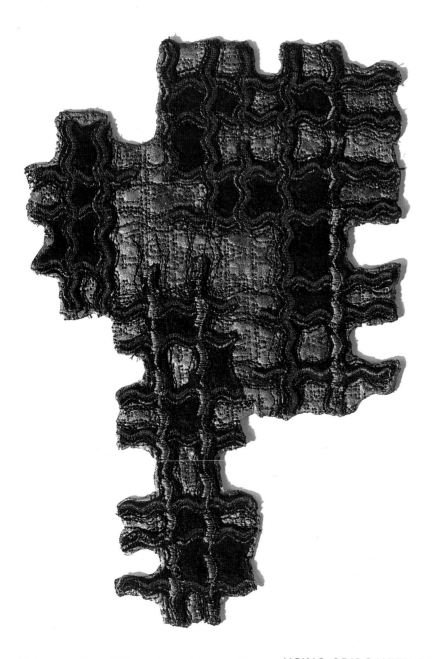

A twin-needle grid, worked using an automatic pattern, was stitched on black felt and cut out, and holes were cut in places. It was applied to a decorated fabric and overstitched.

This method could be extended by working built-in patterns between and over the motifs instead of free machining. It will still be necessary to work several layers of machining to anchor the stitching.

Fig. 40 shows letters applied to a base of water-soluble fabric with a twin-needle grid stitched over the top. Additional stitching – for example, lines of smaller letters – could be worked over this.

USING GRIDS WITH PATCHES

Grids can be a useful way of organizing patches. They can either be stitched directly on to the background fabric or they can be stitched first and then cut out and applied, with or without patches on top of them. They are most effective when used with a twin needle and built-in patterns. Use stabilizer behind thin fabrics or exploit the puckers as a feature of the texture. Use a size 2 or 3 twin needle and the appropriate setting on your machine.

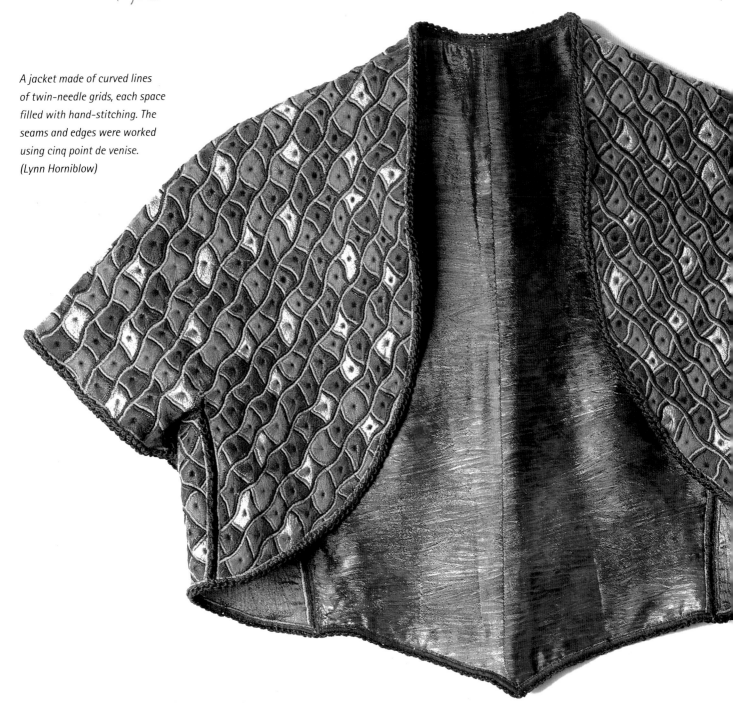

A jacket made of curved lines of twin-needle grids, each space filled with hand-stitching. The seams and edges were worked using cinq point de venise. (Lynn Horniblow)

Try satin stitch or satin stitch auto-patterns – either the 9mm (³⁄₈in) ones or some of the larger edging patterns – or work freely by swinging the fabric from side to side to make irregular curves. Adjust the stitch length or the balance to change the density as you wish. Use the quilting bar to keep lines parallel to each other, although the spacing can be regular or irregular. Widely spaced lines can be cut up and woven together, or have other strips woven through the holes.

When you are stitching grids, try some of the following:

- Work all the horizontal lines and then all vertical ones, or stitch them alternately to give a woven effect.

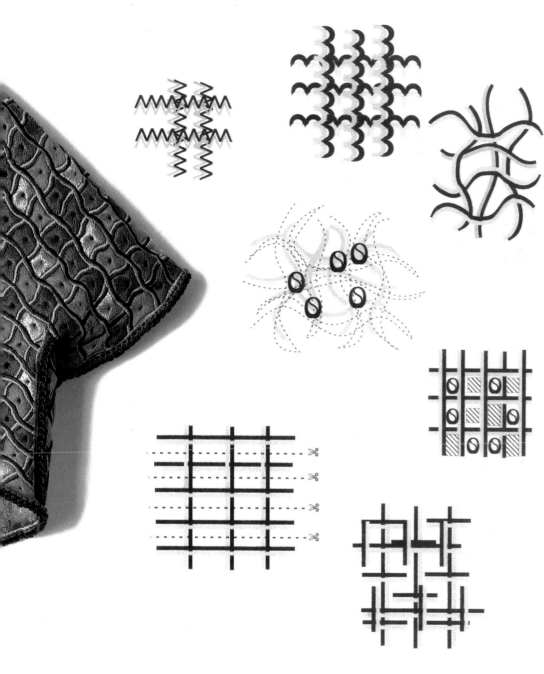

Fig. 41

Twin-needle grids can be stitched freely with the foot off or using the built-in patterns with the foot on. Even if you have the foot on, the fabric can be swung from side to side to give curved lines of stitching and the stitching can be built up in layers. Holes can be cut in the spaces, or patches can be applied to the fabric. Alternatively, the grids can be cut into smaller sections and applied to an embroidered background.

- Work in two different colours, or use metallic or polyester threads on manmade fabrics and then decorate with transfer paints.
- Cut out the holes or fill in spaces with free running stitch or whip stitch.
- Work the grid on water-soluble fabric and then stitch spiders' webs in the holes.
- Use the grid as one large piece, or cut it into smaller pieces and place them on a pre-stitched background.

Other patches, such as flowers or geometric shapes, can be applied on top of the grid, at the intersections or in the spaces, or they can be wrapped over and around the bars.

The cushion is made from the Husqvarna Orchidea motifs shown in the photograph on page 60. These were applied to a background of zapped fabrics, with the edges turned under. A border was worked around them using automatic patterns with an altered tension, which allowed the metallic bobbin thread to show. The edges were made from strips of folded buttonholes.

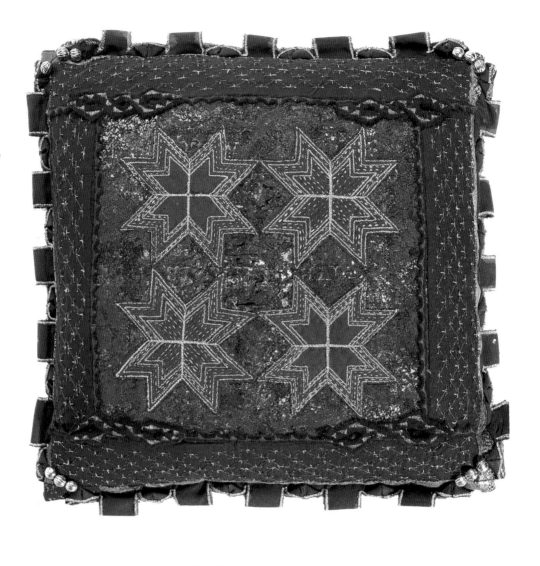

Fig. 42

A thick thread or a bundle of threads can be couched by hand to secure a patch to a fabric. It is better to attach the patch before working the couching.

HAND-STITCHING AND HEMMING

If you have worked a patch on a fabric that is likely to fray and you do not want to use massed stitches to apply it to the background, the edges can be turned under and the patch can be hemmed or stitched to the background in the usual way. The patches on the cushion cover shown have been made in this way. The background for the cushion centre is made from layers of stitch-ing and heat-treated fabrics, as described in the Backgrounds section. The patches used are from the quilting card of a sewing machine with an embroidery unit and have been stitched on to cotton.

The motifs should be cut out following the original outlines but not too close to the stitching. Raw edges can be treated with fray check if necessary and folded to the

'Swinging Sixties', a panel by Cornelia Gilham, is a record of the 1960s in digitized motifs, some stitched directly on the background and some applied.

inside before being applied to the background by hand or machine, using straight stitch around the edges.

COUCHING

Couching can be used to edge patches, and a variety of threads or strips of fabric is suitable for this method. The thread or yarn to be used for couching is stitched around the edge of the motif, and another thread is used to secure both the patch and the edging yarn. The stitch used to secure the couched thread could itself be decorative – chain stitch or fly stitch, for example – and several rows of this could be worked with couching techniques.

8. Painting after Stitching

FABRIC PAINTS

The idea of painting your work after spending all that time stitching may seem a strange one, but excellent results can be achieved, ranging from a subtle jacquard effect to almost a cloth-of-gold if metallic paints are used.

Suitable paints include silk paints, which give a soft feel to the material, or fabric paints, which can be thinned down if desired. Even acrylic paints can be used, although these do stiffen the fabric and can cover the stitching too much. This may not matter if you have made a panel or wall-hanging, but acrylics would not be suitable if you wanted to make a soft drape. Metallic paints are available in a range of colours – silver, bronze, copper or gold – and they can be obtained ready-mixed or made up by being mixed with a suitable fabric medium, such as Liquitex or Ormaline, with bronze powders, which often gives a richer mix. (Remember to wear a mask when you use powdered metallic paints so that you do not inhale any particles.) It is also possible, of course, to add highlights to previously painted stitching.

Follow the steps outlined below to achieve the best results.

1 Stitch your fabric. All-over stitching can be used to attach the patches, or the motifs produced in the Slips and Patches section can be painted before they are applied to a background fabric. Interesting effects can be achieved if both background and patches are painted together after stitching.

2 Use a neutral or pale background fabric and stitch with a pale thread. Rayon thread gives good results, but experiment with other threads and different weights for a range of effects.

3 Place the fabric on a waterproof surface and apply the paint. If you want the colours to merge it might help if the work is lightly sprayed with water before painting. Thicker paints will need to be pushed well into the stitching, so use a short-bristled brush and a punching action. This technique will also be necessary if you use metallic paints.

4 If you are using metallic paints to create highlights, let the painted fabric dry before drawing an almost dry brush of metallic paint across it. Build up the paint slowly so that it does not form blobs. This method could also be used when Xpandaprint has been used with the stitching (see page 14).

WAX EMULSION AND BRONZE POWDERS

Acrylic wax can be mixed with a small quantity of bronze powder. (Remember to wear a mask when you do this.) You can vary the amount of powder that is added to the wax to give a range of effects, from a light sheen to a much heavier, metallic look. This is a good way of knocking back over-bright colours, particularly silk paints, which can sometimes be a little too vibrant.

Prepare the stitching and paint as outlined above, then mix the powder with the wax and paint over the painted stitching. Leave to dry thoroughly.

OPPOSITE

A wall-hanging based on fossil studies. Heavily stitched on polycotton with patches applied, it was burned with a soldering iron, painted with acrylic paints and highlighted with metallic waxes.

The colour sticks produced by ChromaCoal are soft, dry pastels, which can also be used over stitching. Just rub the chalky stick over the work and use a heat gun to set the colour. Do not allow the ChromaCoal to get too hot; it is better to apply a slow, steady warmth and to hold the heat gun a little away from the material. A very colourful effect can be produced in this way, and the colour sticks work particularly well over dark, crunchy stitching. The chalk in the sticks is crumbly, so apply the colour lightly and build it up in layers. One colour can be applied and heat-set before another is added over the top. The results can be seen in the photograph on page 38.

EMBOSSING POWDERS

Embossing powders, which are often used with rubber stamps to give a raised, highlighted look, are widely available in craft shops. They can be used on top of stitching if an adhesive such as PVA is applied to the surface. Stitch and paint as before, using a paint, such as silk paint, that can be heated safely.

When the paint is dry dab a small amount of adhesive sparsely over the surface that you want to highlight. Immediately sprinkle over the embossing powder. Turn over the work and tap the excess powder on to a sheet of paper. Shoot this back into the pot to save waste. Use a heat gun to heat the powder; you need not wait until the adhesive is dry. The embossing powder will bubble and melt to form a crusty surface.

The powders are available in metallic shades or in a range of plain colours, and they can be mixed to give exciting results. Gold or copper used with verdigris or greenish-blue powders will look like old metal. Experiment with different powders on stitches.

9. Making Three-dimensional Pieces

Backgrounds and patches can be combined to form three-dimensional pieces of work. These could take the form of containers, masks or fans, or they could be incorporated into the background to form undulating waves or shapes within a wall-hanging or panel.

APPLYING MOTIFS TO PRE-FORMED SHAPES

A material such as thermoplastic foam, can be heated in an oven and moulded into a shape while it is still warm. Patches can be applied to the shaped material, usually by hand-stitching. It is also possible to stitch one of the backgrounds over the moulded shape and then apply patches and further stitching over the top. Masks are an obvious

Book made from thermoplastic foam. The foam was shaped over two bottles while it was still warm. Patches of water-soluble stitching were applied, and the 'leaves' were free machined, also on dissolvable fabric.

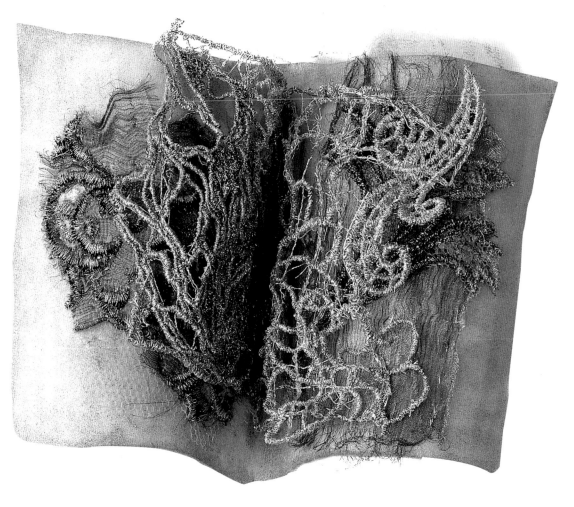

BELOW **Fig. 43**

Wireform can be stitched as it is or when it is covered with fabric. Holes can be cut into it, and cord satin

stitched to mark a fold. The mesh can be folded or bent in any direction, or two pieces can be joined with lacing to make a sharp corner.

OPPOSITE

A vessel made from transparent fabrics sandwiched between Wireform and stitched with automatic patterns. The shapes were cut out, edged with leather thong and folded.

item, but the technique is also useful for containers, and many other shaped items can be produced. The following technique was used to create thermoplastic foam 'books' with applied motifs and water-soluble fabric 'pages'.

1   Cut the moulding material to a suitable size and shape and put it in a pre-heated oven, following the manufacturer's instructions.

2   Take the foam from the oven and immediately press it down over two bottles to give the correct shape to the covers. The material cools quickly and retains its shape, if you have made a mistake and want to change the shape, simply reheat the foam and try again.

3   Take some previously stitched patches. The ones illustrated directional were stitched on sheer fabric with water-soluble fabric underneath to strengthen it. The patch is first stitched to the front of the cover using a strong needle and a stab stitch motion, up and down, through the cover. Further hand-

stitching can be added to hold the fabric flat.

4   The motif for the inside cover is applied in the same manner, but, because the stitches will show on the previously stitched outer cover, a toning thread should be used and the stitching on the outer should be as unobtrusive as possible. Repeat for the back cover.

5   Attach the inner pages. These were made by free machining on water-soluble fabric with wire around the edges to hold the shape.

WIREFORM

Take care when you use this material – it has sharp edges. Wireform is the tradename of a lightweight wire mesh that is available in a variety of thicknesses and patterns. It has obvious uses for modelling fabrics because it can be folded, pleated and woven and it holds its shape. Use a strong needle, which should be kept for use with metal and wire. You should be able to use your sewing machine to stitch on the wire.

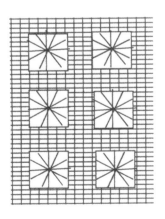
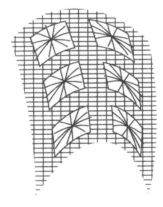
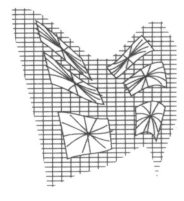

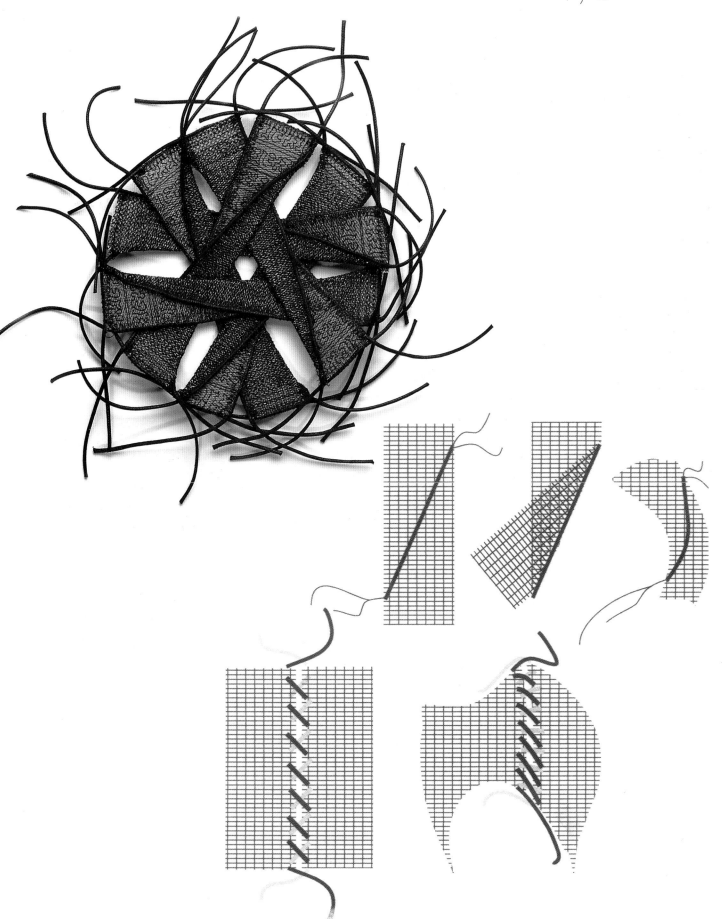

Fabric can be laid on top of or under the mesh, or you can make a mesh sandwich. Attractive effects can be obtained with sheer fabrics and layers of net or pre-stitched fabric. Stitch with auto-patterns in a toning or contrasting thread and bend the resulting material into shape when stitching is complete. The lines along which the Wireform is to be bent can be marked with a row of satin stitch or close zigzag stitch, which will give a good, crisp bend. So that you know the position of the lines beforehand, make a paper model to work out the angles and shapes. Corners can cause problems, but they can be cut. Alternatively, the edges can be folded in or allowed to fan out on the inside or outside.

For a crisp, regular shape, such as a box, the pieces can be cut out to the required size first. The sides can then be finished with an edging stitch on the machine, folded up and laced together by hand using a heavier thread.

You could also use Wireform to make up separate elements – varied shapes that could be bent over a wire for decorative collars, for example, or an applied decoration to panel, container or mask. Before you begin work, think about how you will deal with the edges, because, if the piece is to be worn next to the skin, they will have to be bound so that the wire does not scratch you.

Vessels can be made by applying fabric to Wireform and cutting out suitable shapes, which can then be folded or bent and joined. The pieces illustrated have thong stitched along the edges and fold lines. The ends of the thongs continue beyond the shape to form decorative swirls.

Wireform can also be used as a grid with holes cut out. Patterns worked on water-soluble fabric could be stitched over the holes and the backing fabric dissolved. The piece

TOP

A container made from transparent fabrics sandwiched between Wireform and stitched with automatic patterns. The shapes were cut out, edged with leather thong and folded.

RIGHT

Small tiles and shapes made from fabric placed over Wireform were manipulated and hand-stitched to create a design on a painted Bondaweb background.

These samples were made from water-soluble paper on Wireform, painted with acrylics and highlighted with embossing powder. The intention was to produce a stitchable fabric resembling metal.

A Celtic pattern, distorted on the computer, was scanned and stitched a number of times using the Janome 9000. The pieces were cut out and the edges burned, and then sewn together.

BELOW

A bowl was made from cut-out strips of a large Pfaff Creative 7570 pattern, which were woven and wrapped around wire that had been formed into the shape of a bowl.

could then be bent into whatever shape you wish. It could be covered in fabric and made into little tiles – squares, diamonds or rectangles – which are pinched and pleated in the centre to create a raised area. They could then be applied to a background to make a border or arranged to form a central design. It could be pleated and laced or pinched into frills and used to edge a panel.

Strips of stitched Wireform could be woven to form a larger piece, which could then be bent into shape. Additional braids, threads and so on could be incorporated in the weaving.

You could use built-in patterns or free machining to stitch water-soluble paper (not water-soluble fabric; see page 91) to Wireform. If you apply a resist – nail var-

nish, for example, or Pebeo Gel Crystals (gel paint used by glass painters) – to some areas of the water-soluble paper, they will not dissolve with the rest of the paper. Think carefully about creating linking areas with the resist and remember that anything that is not painted will wash away. Dry the piece thoroughly and then decorate it with embossing ink and powder, which will give an attractive 'old metal' effect.

STITCHING FELT PATCHES TO FORM SHAPES

Patches can be stitched heavily on a fabric like felt, which is a useful material because the patches can be cut out close to the outlines and the fabric will not fray. The pieces can then be joined and used to make bowls, containers and frames. Because felt is so flexible it can be easily manipulated, particularly after stitching, but the stitching must be heavy because it will be supporting the structure.

Before you join pieces of felt consider the shape of the overall structure you want to achieve and the shape of the individual pieces. You should also think about the edges of the pieces: they could be cut and left, machined using an edging stitch, beaded, bound, couched or hand-stitched.

When you have decided on the shape you want to create, make a pattern from paper and staple it together to make sure that the individual pieces work together. Then stitch each element on felt using free machine

techniques or automatic machine embroidery. Join the pieces together as the pattern suggests, manipulating them as you wish.

CREATING SHAPES FROM STITCHED FELT STRIPS

The method you use to join pieces of felt will have a major impact on the general appearance of the finished item and also to its shape. For example, the edges could be joined by hand – by stab stitching with a thick thread or buttonhole stitch, for example – and this gives a very firm edge, which helps to support the shape. Working buttonhole stitch around the edges of the patches would lend itself to a lacing technique to join the pieces.

If felt strips, decorated with built-in pattern, are cut so that they gradually decrease in length, they can be manipulated to create a bowl.

1 Stitch lines of built-in pattern onto some felt. Use one large pattern or two or three patterns massed together.

The piece was made from felt strips, stitched with automatic patterns and pulled into a curved shape by stitch. The metal 'petals' in the centre were hammered into shape.

Fig. 44
When two strips of felt of different lengths are buttonholed together – ease the longer strip while you stitch – quite sharp curves can be created.

OPPOSITE

Fig. 45

*Design for a piece of stitching,
which could be used to make a
necklace.*

Fig. 46

*Design for a small panel or book
cover, which could be made
using woven strips of stitched
background fabrics with flower
motifs applied.*

*A bed-head by Pat Frost. The
background was stitched with
automatic patterns, and the
strap was worked freely on
water-soluble fabric.*

2 Cut the felt into five strips, so that the
longest strip is about 10cm (4in) long
and the others decrease in length by
about 15mm (⅝in) per strip.

3 Use buttonhole stitch to attach the
strips together, pulling the shorter one
into the longer one so that the piece
curves.

4 Pull the shorter end under at the
bottom to accentuate the curve.

The stitched strips could be formed into
petals or joined together to make a circular
bowl.

WEAVING STRIPS THROUGH A WIRE FRAME

Large patterns stitched on felt strips could
be cut out close to the stitching and wound
through a frame made from gardening
wire. The underside of the stitching will be
visible and will look particularly attractive
if you use metallic thread in the bobbin.
Use pliers to join lengths of wire to make a
bowl, for example. Wire could also be bent
to make picture or mirror frames. When
you have made the basic framework, patterned strips can be woven up and down

through the wire; catch them with stab
stitch occasionally to hold them in position. The wire framework could also be
wrapped around with the stitched strip, and
then further large patterned pieces could be
added to it.

Other methods for joining strips to make
bowls or containers include:

- Accentuating seams in the fabric of the
  patch that is used as a fold line.
- Folding the patch and machining the
  outside of the fold.
- Lacing together pieces by means of
  eyelets made in each patch.
- Laying the patch on water-soluble
  fabric and stitching over to join them.

As this section has shown, there are ways in
which patches can be applied to backgrounds and then used to create larger
items. Only a few of the many possible
methods can be included here, so do experiment and find many more of your own. The
ways in which backgrounds and motifs are
created makes them especially appropriate
for this type of experimentation.

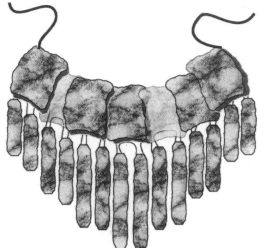

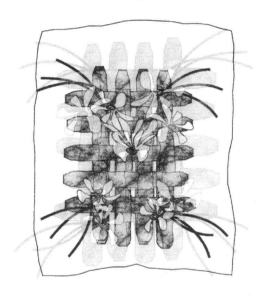

'Cat', a panel by Maureen Humphries. Each cat was made using a digitized design and then applied to a background.

Chapter Four

Edges, Tassels and Trimmings

10. Edges

The way a piece of work is finished is as important as any other aspect of its production and should be considered from the outset, not treated as an afterthought. Many of the techniques that have been discussed in earlier chapters can also be used for finishing, including the use of decorative patterns and patches (slips). In this final part of the book we look at some decorative edgings, the use of tabs – either to suspend work or as an integral part of the decoration – and the use of the feet and attachments that come with a machine and can be used for cords, braids and edgings.

The first factor to consider is whether the piece should have straight, curved or shaped edges. Should those edges be smooth and finished with, for example, hemming stitch, or rough and finished by burning or tearing methods? Will the piece be mounted, framed or hung up? If the work is to be merged into a larger embroidery it could be heavily stitched to integrate it or the edge could be used as part of the larger pattern.

STITCHED EDGES

Using a zigzag or satin stitch over the edges of a piece of embroidery gives a neat finish, but think carefully about the type and colour of thread you use – the thread could contrast or tone with the main stitching, for example. There are many other stitches that

RIGHT

A sampler of machine-embroidered edges.

could be used, including some of the decorative ones, and ribbons, braids or narrow cords could be couched down under a decorative stitch to provide a more solid edging. A highly decorative edging can be made from a chain of crochet:

1   Use double knitting wool and crochet a chain by forming a loop, passing the hook through the loop to pick up the wool behind it and pulling it back through the hoop. Continue until the chain is the required length.
2   Set the machine to zigzag with a normal top and bottom tension. Make the zigzag just wider than the crocheted chain.
3   Using the braiding foot, gently ease the chain through the foot, stitching quite slowly. Do not pull the chain through; just guide it on its way. The stitches will jump over the bumps in the chain, leaving an attractive bobbled effect.
4   Use the sewing machine to couch the crocheted chain to the edge of the piece using more zigzag stitches.

MACHINE COUCHING

There are many yarns that can be used to make an edging for a piece of work, and the couching technique that you use could be bold to make it stand out or subtle so that it becomes an integral part of the edge. A firm yarn, such as gimp or a length of thong, also makes a good edging. Use one of the following methods:

*   Place the yarn on the edge of the work, pin it in position and use one of the satin stitch patterns – scallop works particularly well – over the cord and on to the main fabric.
*   Use fine cord, string or gimp double. Place two lengths side by side and hold them together with a three-step zigzag stitch. Hold it to the edge of a fabric with a built-in pattern or another row of three-step zigzag.
*   Use extra cords to make a firmer edging. These could be stitched with multiple rows of zigzag before they are placed on the edge and decorated with a built-in pattern in satin stitch.

The idea of using several cords to make a firm edging could be extended to create even heavier edgings, which could be couched to the piece. For example, strips of felt, wound into fat tubes and wrapped with overstitched bands of plain fabric and bands of cut-out satin stitches, would make a good edging for a suitable piece of work.

Fig. 47

Many different stitched edges can be worked on a machine, including **(a)** *a cord zigzagged to the edge with an overlocking foot;* **(b)** *small beads attached to a corded edge;* **(c)** *a cord secured with freely stitched cross-hatching;* **(d)** *multiple cords attached with zigzag stitching;* **(e)** *a cord attached to an edge before being bound with transparent fabric (so that it is still visible) and the edge secured with an automatic pattern; and* **(f)** *long and short stitch (available on some machines) used to cover the edge with a second row worked as decoration.*

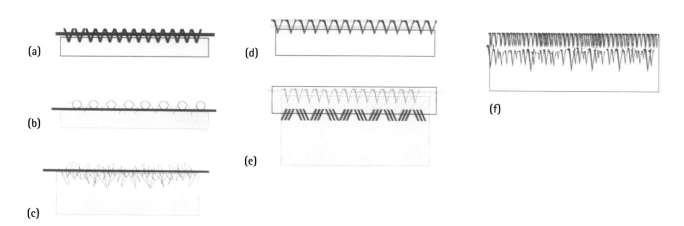

(a)

(b)

(c)

(d)

(e)

(f)

Fig. 48

The overlocking foot with a metal bar, which prevents the stitching from curling the edge of the fabric.

Fig. 49

The pearls 'n' piping foot (sometimes called the knit edge foot or the bulky edge foot) has a groove underneath so that thick cords or strung beads can be couched.

You could even stuff pieces of drinking straw with more straw. Slit one straw down its length and flatten two or three other straws, which you can insert into the first straw. The straws could be decorated with any sort of paint, and some of the texturing materials could create attractive effects, too. When the straws are dry, wrap them in cut-out strips of patterns, stitched on felt or heavy interfacing. They could then be couched to the edges of a piece of work. This would make a decorative, but quite heavy, edging, which would not be suitable for light, lacy work.

BOUND EDGES

Edges can be bound by stitching a strip of fabric along the edge, with right sides together. The fabric strip is then turned to the back and secured by hand or machine. Suitable fabrics for bindings include plain fabric, net and organza, stitched with built-in patterns, and ribbons and braids.

A detail of a bag showing satin stitched edges.

ALTERNATIVE FEET
Overlocking Foot

Fig. 48

The overlocking foot has a metal bar on the right-hand side instead of a second toe, and this allows you to work zigzag or satin stitch on the very edge of a piece of fabric or ribbon. The foot stops the fabric curling and makes it much easier to stitch right to the edge.

PEARLS 'N' PIPING FOOT

Fig. 49

This type of foot allows thick cord to pass underneath it. Different machine manufacturers call the foot by different names, but they perform the same function. The foot allows you to stitch over knotted strips of fabric or even quite large beads previously strung on heavy thread. The beads can be attached to the edge of the piece as they pass under the foot. Alternatively, if you wanted to create a beaded edge, the beads could be threaded on wire and then more wire could be wrapped around and over them. There are some attractive enamelled wires available in good colours or you could use florist's wire.

BURNED EDGES

When you are burning edges do make sure that you take all necessary precautions. If you are using a soldering iron, for example, always use it so that it points away from your body and it is advisable to wear a respirator and not just a mask. Carry out the

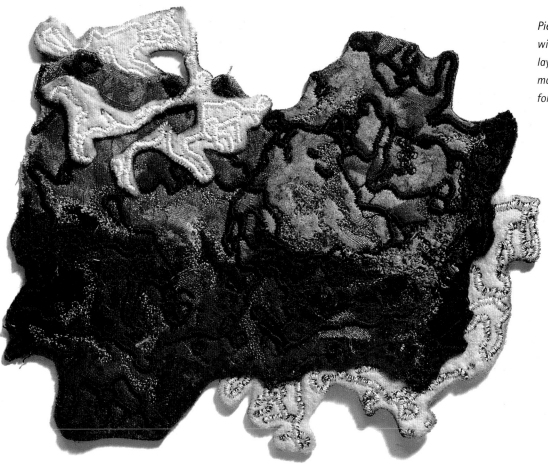

Pieces of stitching, cut out and with burned edges, built up in layers with added free machining and granite stitch for texture.

work on a metal tray or another heatproof surface away from flammable materials, and always test with a small piece of material before you begin.

As long as you are careful, using a soldering iron or heat gun can be good fun. Many fabrics, such as sheer materials and velvets, can be welded together with a soldering iron simply by pressing it through the layers, which creates a sealed, fray-proof edging. Other fabrics will give a ragged edge, which can be very attractive. Polycotton burns particularly well, and it is not as rough as cotton but is not too smooth for some interesting effects.

If you are using felt and some sheer fabrics it is possible to use a heat gun on the edge of a piece of work by masking off the main area with damp fabric. The heat can then be directed to the exposed area only. This can be particularly effective if you have used acrylic felt. Alternatively, strips of felt with patterns stitched on them could be heated with the heat gun and then plaited, twisted or woven together before being used as a border.

LACY EDGES

Light, delicate edges can be created by placing water-soluble fabric under the edge of the main work and continuing the stitching over the edge and on to the fabric. You could use free machine techniques or you could make use of the built-in patterns in your machine. Alternatively, the water-soluble fabric could have been previously stitched with suitable motifs, and these

A fan constructed from sprayed garden wire and Wireform, which was covered with fabric and stitched using parts of a frame motif from the Bernina lettering facility. The edges were made from heavy stitching on net, and water-soluble fabric was used to edge the net and provide a finish.

could now be overstitched to incorporate them into the main work. Remember to stitch a grid on the water-soluble fabric before you use built-in patterns or motifs, or the stitches may unravel when the fabric is dissolved. Snippets of fabric could be included in the stitching to give slightly more weight.

HAND–STITCHED EDGES

Couching techniques could be used to hand-stitch a variety of yarns or fabric strips to the edges of your work. Experiment with stitches. Random cross stitch, chain stitch and so on could all be used with a heavy yarn to make a decorative edge. Strips of knotted, stitched or cut-out fabric could be applied, and stuffed ribbons or rolled fabric could also be used.

USING PATCHES AS EDGES

Patches, made using the embroidery unit or by free machining a motif, can be used as edgings. Before you use them, however, look at the overall design of the piece. Could the patches be folded over the edge? Will they form part of a field and border design where the border is defined by the patches? If so, will the border be straight or will it flow into the field (main) part of the work?

Patches could be made from vanishing muslin, partly dissolved and painted. These might be stitched as formal or geometric shapes, or they could be used as stitched patches that echo motifs from the main embroidery. Patches stitched on water-soluble fabric could be used in the same way. Motifs made by both methods may have to be applied to a heavier fabric, such as felt or pelmet-weight interfacing, to make them sturdy enough, although, if they are carefully applied, they could be used alone to give a delicate look to a piece of fine work.

Shaped patches can be used to create a particularly interesting edge. Made from a firm material, such as felt, they can be cut close to the stitching and used on the edges of a piece of embroidery or, if they are the right shape, as a means of suspending the work.

Folding the motifs or manipulating them into shapes offers further possibilities for creating unusual edgings. For example, leaf shapes could be stitched on felt and cut out. Arrange them over the edge of the piece by overlapping and stitching by hand or machine. You could try the same approach with letters or free-machined

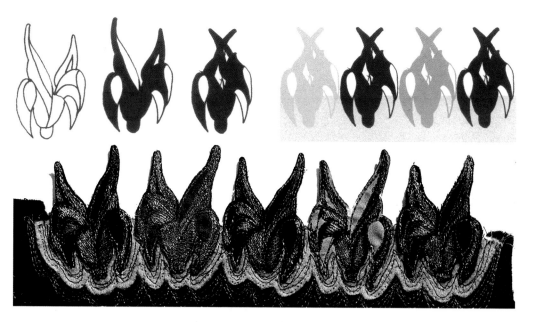

Fig. 51
Small patches can be used to decorate an edge. The points of these leaves were crossed over each other to give a three-dimensional shape that would work well on vessels or bags.

LEFT
Leaves, part of a pattern on the Deco 500, were applied and stitched to the edge of a fabric. Free machining was added in contour lines to soften the transition from the solid stitching to the bare fabric.

OPPOSITE BOTTOM LEFT
Fig. 50
Hand-worked stitches, such as cross stitch, chain stitch or straight stitch, can be used to cover edges of embroidered pieces or of patches applied to backgrounds.

shapes, and small patterns from an embroidery card could also be used in this way.

BLENDING EDGES

Incorporating previously stitched borders or motifs into a piece requires thought, and the background of both pieces must be especially carefully assessed. For instance, it is relatively easy to merge a patch into work that contains heavy free machining but it is more difficult if the background is painted or lightly machined.

Braids or lines of pattern could be used. You could use the colour of lines of straight stitch to merge two divergent areas, or you could try hand-stitching techniques, such as adding lines of running stitch, which could be used around the edges of the piece to be blended in.

Patches blended as described above can also be used to decorate the spines of books or to make borders. The following idea for a book spine came from a spiral-bound book and uses built-in patterns and patches and machine-embroidered motifs.

1 Cut a piece of felt to the correct size for the book. Mark the position of the spine and stitch along its length using three or four open decorative patterns. Vary the thickness of the thread, change direction and pile the patterns on top of each other to give good coverage.

2 Stitch motifs on felt and cut out. They should be wider than the spine and should be placed at right-angles to the stitching. Make sure they extend over the spine and on to the front and back covers so that they stiffen the spine and look as if they are enclosing it.

3 Work straight stitches down the length of the spine to bed in the patches and blend them with the background. Use straight stitch free machining to attach the overlapping motifs to the front and back covers.

4 Decorate the cover with tassels or buttonholed rings and use cords and braids (see page 123).

This method could be adapted and used to create borders for wall-hangings or panels for bags.

The spine of a book. Built-in cable patterns were stitched on a dyed fabric that had been backed with felt. Larger cable patterns were scanned and stitched using the Deco 600 and applied, secured with massed lines of straight stitching. Cut-out cables were plaited and applied to the centre of the spine, with wrapped rings representing a spiral binding.

Fig. 52
Patches can be secured to a background and blended in by using automatic patterns or straight stitching with the foot on.

Long buttonholes were worked on a fabric and cut. The fabric was folded in half to make tabs, and more stitching and beads were added.

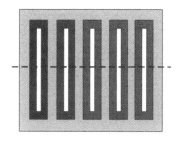 

Fig. 53
Extra-long buttonholes worked on the edge of the fabric can be folded in half to make tabs. They can be left as they are, alternate tabs can be folded back or tassels can be used to decorate them.

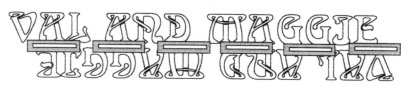
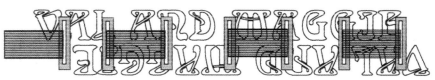

Fig. 54
Buttonholes worked over automatic patterns or letters can be threaded with ribbon or cord.

BUTTONHOLED EDGES

Most sewing machines have a buttonhole foot, and many models have an option that allows you to enter the size of the buttonhole into the machine's memory so that they are all exactly the same size. Some machines have a slot in which the button is held and measured, and most offer the facility to produce different styles of buttonhole. Consult your machine's manual and try the different styles.

Buttonholes make excellent edging strips. A band of buttonholes can be folded in half and stitched into the seams of a cushion cover when you are making it up. At the corners the tabs formed can be pulled forwards and caught down with a few stitches. You could add some beads as additional decoration, or you could use cut-out satin stitch strips, twisted together and threaded through the buttonhole. A battlement-style edging could be created by folding down alternate tabs.

Another possibility would be to make a series of buttonholes in stitched fabric and thread plain strips or ribbon through them, or you could use lettering on either side of the buttonhole band.

When they are stitched on felt, buttonholes can be cut out and applied to a backing strip to form a border. You could run further

*A variety of edging techniques
displayed on luggage labels. The
detail of each one was written
on the reverse for easy
reference.*

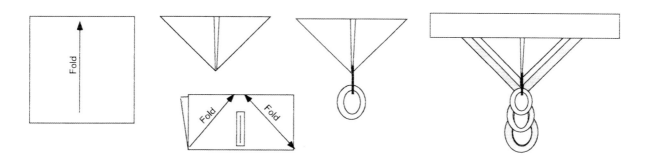

cords or stitched strips through them or you could work them at random on a base fabric, with cut-out buttonholes applied over them. Long, cut-out buttonholes might form tabs, which could be stitched over a base to allow further bands of stitched patterns to be threaded through them. Suitable motifs could also be threaded through these strips, which can also be used as tabs by stitching a row of long buttonholes, folding them in half and adding tassels to the ends.

Another use for buttonholes is to include them in prairie points.

1 Work the buttonhole across a rectangle of fabric that has been folded in half.
2 Both lower corner points are folded up behind with the buttonhole to form the point.
3 Attach a tassel or a ring through the buttonhole.

Multiple prairie points made in this way can be built up in layers. The scrolling built-in pattern can be used to good effect here. The same pattern can be stitched on a long strip, encased by decorated ribbons, as shown in Fig. 55.

ABOVE **Fig. 55**

If buttonholes are worked in the angle of prairie points rings or tassels can be suspended from them.

Prairie points made from fabric were decorated with an automatic pattern, and a buttonhole was worked on each point. Tassels were added to hang from the points, and additional stitching was worked to blend the colours.

11. Tassels, Cords and Braids

Seashell motifs from a Janome card were stitched on felt in different sizes, cut out and manipulated to form two tassels.

BELOW LEFT
Large letters, either built into the Bernina 180 or scanned and stitched on the Janome 9000, were used to cover the tassel heads.

TASSELS

It is possible to make fantastic tassel heads by using motifs from the embroidery cards or the larger built-in patterns provided with the machine, and the most unlikely motifs can often be manipulated to form interesting shapes. Free-machined motifs can also be used here, but you should consider their shape and size carefully before using them in this way. This also applies when using the machine scanner or software. Heavy stitching works best on felt so that the design can be cut out without fraying, and felt also has the advantage of holding a shape well when it is manipulated.

You will need at least two motifs to form a tassel head. If the design is reversed – remember that you can use the work bobbin-side up to reverse it – it will make a back-to-back tassel head and the skirt can be threaded through to make a long, thin, elegant tassel. Stitch the motifs together by machine with a narrow zigzag or by hand with buttonhole stitch, which could be beaded.

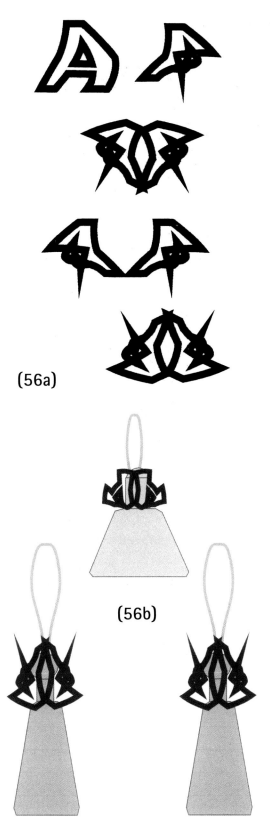

(56a)

(56b)

To make a chunkier tassel stitch three motifs, one slightly smaller than the other two. Stitch on felt and cut out the shapes, then take some time to manipulate the pieces. Pin them together and twist, stretch and manipulate them to form a three-dimensional shape. There are several possible ways of joining them: you could stitch them together with the seams outside, add beads or metal thread, possibly purl-purl, or couch down threads along the seam line.

TASSELS FROM LETTERS

If your machine will stitch large letters these can be stitched on felt and cut out to make tassels. Otherwise, use the widest possible satin stitch to form letters more freely by drawing the shapes first. Remember that the bobbin thread will show, so wind the bobbin accordingly,

The 'legs' of letters like A, K or X can be distorted, pulled back on themselves and stitched together to make new shapes. If you choose P or B other letters can be pulled through the holes. If large beads are used as a base the letters can enclose them, with spiky edges formed from the straight areas. The best way is to sit down with a handful of cut-out letters and play around with them. It is surprising what can be achieved in this way.

Net is another good fabric for these tassels because the straight stitch gives it a slightly jagged effect. Like felt, it can be cut close to the stitching but the finished tassel will be a little lighter.

PATTERN-WRAPPED CORDS

Use stitched strips cut out from a suitable fabric, such as felt, to wrap around heavy string or piping cord. Cut-out felt strips could also be plaited together to make braids

Fig. 56a and 56b

Letters and other shapes can be distorted on the computer or in the sewing machine scanner to make interesting shapes for tassel heads. They can be sewn in pairs or in groups of three or even four, and the edges can be decorated with tiny beads.

OPPOSITE BELOW RIGHT
Tassels, made from machine stitching on felt, were folded and manipulated and then stitched to the tassel heads. The red tassel was made from three large leaf patterns built into the Pfaff 7570; the silver tassel used a pattern on a Pfaff embroidery card; the rust-coloured tassel used a leaf pattern from the Deco 500; and the red and grey tassels used patterns on a Bernina embroidery card.

Automatic patterns were stitched on to felt and cut into strips. The strips were wound around thick piping cord and hand wrapped to secure them.

and cords. Experiment with some of the larger patterns. Strips of built-in pattern, cut out close to the stitching, could be twisted together in pairs.

MACHINE-WRAPPED CORDS
Braiding Foot

Fig. 57

The braiding foot (known as the cording foot on some machines) has a hole through which cord can pass. This foot is indispensable if you are covering string or yarn with stitching. The tunnel underneath means that the cord is not squashed.

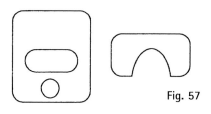

Fig. 57

To make wrapped cords use the braiding foot, which has a central hole in the front and a 'tunnel' underneath, a pearls 'n' piping foot or the foot you use to sew pieces of knitting together, because these control the cord. If you are using a sewing machine with snap-on feet, remove the foot and make use of the bottom of the bar to stop the cord jumping about too much.

You can wrap string, knitting yarns, embroidery threads, piping cord, raffia, twisted cords, wire, strips of fabric or tights, or knitting ribbon – plain or stuffed – or previously stitched using the looping foot.

Set the sewing machine to normal tension if you are using coloured threads, or to loose top tension and a large needle if you are using metallic threads. If you set a very loose top tension, the top thread will wrap right around the cord, and this could mean that you do not need metallic thread on the bobbin. The teeth should be left up. It is possible to use no feet at all, or use a quilting foot and drop the teeth, but this requires more control on your part. Set the zigzag to its widest width, even if you are only covering a narrow yarn, because it is easier to see the stitching and the stitches will pull in tightly as you move along. Use stitch length 1–2.

To cover the yarn, hold it (and the two ends of thread) at the back of the needle with your left hand, and hold the yarn you are covering in front of the needle with your right hand. Stitch, keeping a firm tension on the yarn all the time so that it is not dragged down into

Fig. 58

Previously strung beads can be attached to a cord while you are stitching it. The beads move out of the way of the needle, which never seems to hit one.

the hole in the needle plate and gently pulling it through. Wrap the finished cord around your left hand as it grows, removing it every so often and starting again.

If you are covering long lengths of yarn, wrap the finished cord from time to time around a large wooden bobbin or piece of card to control it. Do not attempt to cover the cord completely in one journey, but make two or three passes, blending the colours if you are using a variegated thread or using a different colour for each journey. If your thread breaks re-thread the machine and continue, holding the loose threads towards you and covering them as you go.

To add texture you can make lumps or 'beads' by moving the cord back and forth, building up the stitching over a small area to make the lumps. These should be worked on the last journey and can be a different colour from the cord. You can also include small tufts of fabric or threads as you go, or try knotting the cord at intervals. For a stiff cord cover string or a stiff yarn and make more journeys, or use metallic threads, which will produce a stiff cord. To make a softer cord cover soft knitting wool or strips of tights and make fewer journeys using a coloured thread.

For further decoration you can wrap a cord loosely with a metallic thread, or another machine-wrapped cord. You can zigzag pre-strung beads to it, knotting both ends together before you stitch to hold them in place and pushing the beads into position as you sew.

When the cord is finished it can be used as it is for suspending panels or it can be attached to bags, cushion covers or book covers.

To wrap the head or neck of a tassel with a cord, spread a little adhesive – thick PVA

works well – on the narrow end of a wooden tassel mould so that about one-third of the mould is covered. Wind the cord firmly over it, leaving a short tail at the beginning. When the glue is dry, cover another one-third of the mould and wind as before. Complete the remaining winding and leave to dry thoroughly. Cut the cord at the end, leaving a short tail, then glue both ends firmly inside the hole, squashing them as flat as possible.

MACHINE BRAIDS AND BRAIDED FABRICS

The following braids give a different effect from the machine-wrapped cords because they are flatter and lend themselves to manipulation.

Flat Braids

Fig. 59

Sew a number of yarns, threads, narrow ribbons or fabric strips together, working as outlined below, remembering that soft yarns

A tassel with a wooden mould was covered with zigzagged cord. The same cord, tied into Carrick bends, was used as an overskirt. (Jackie Dunn)

Fig. 59
The satin stitch foot is useful because the wide channel underneath it prevents bulky stitches from piling up on top of each other.

will create a more regular braid because each thread is kept in its own channel. Keep all the yarns in a bowl, box or carrier bag on the floor. Work with normal tension at top and bottom and with dropped teeth, using the normal foot. Sew the braid with a plain zigzag stitch set at the widest width. Twist the threads slightly, first clockwise and then anticlockwise, to give a variegated effect.

Round Braids or Cords

Sew a number of yarns, threads, narrow ribbons or fabric strips together using the braiding or pearls 'n' piping foot with a tunnel underneath or the darning foot. Use a zigzag stitch, which will pull the threads into a round cord because of the tension on the thread.

JOINING BRAIDS TOGETHER

Hold the braids even more firmly at the back and the front of the machine to avoid them curving as you sew. If they do curve, pull on one side or the other to straighten them up again. Stitch using one of the following:

- The same elastic stitch, or a fagotting stitch, for joining flat braids.
- The fancy elastic stitch, or a fagotting stitch, which are used for joining butted edges together, for the round braids.
- A built-in pattern.

USING CORDS AND BRAIDS

Cords generally look better when they are massed rather than being thinly spread. You could thread them through eyelets in stitched fabrics or run them through buttonholes. Stitching single raised buttonholes in rows means that you can run cords or braids through them. Eyelets can be used in the same way.

Patches, stitched at each end so that the centre is free, can be used like this too, and

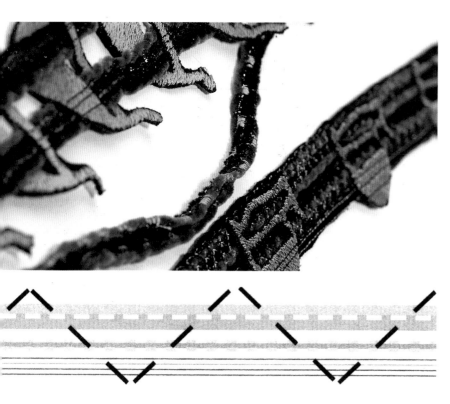

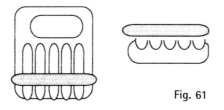

Fig. 60
Stitched braid can be made from a number of yarns.

TOP LEFT
Flat braids were made by stitching threads together with a three-step zigzag. Automatic patterns were then stitched over the top. Celtic letter Ds were scanned and stitched on the Janome 9000 and threaded on to the braids. Straight stitching down the length was worked to hold them in place.

and threads make a soft braid and that stiffer yarns and metal threads, and closer stitching, make a stiffer braid.

1 Use normal tension at top and bottom, teeth up, and use the satin stitch foot.
2 Sew the braid with a stretch stitch, or three-step zigzag, using a long length and the widest width your machine can do.
3 Hold the yarns firmly at the back and front of the machine.

A variation can be made by using the cording foot (which has channels on the top of the foot, each one to hold a thread), which

Fig. 61
The cording (couching) foot holds several yarns in place while they are being couched. The metal flap keeps the yarns in the grooves.

Fig. 61

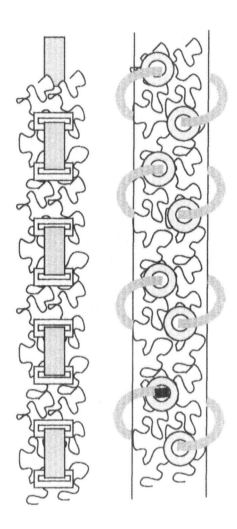

Fig. 62
If buttonholes or eyelets are worked over automatic patterns on water-soluble fabric ribbon or cord can be threaded through after the fabric has been dissolved.

The tassel was made from drawings scanned and stitched into the Deco 500 and sewn together. They were covered with sequins sewn on by hand and edged with cinq point de venise, and bead tassels were attached to the points.
(Lynn Horniblow)

the cord can run underneath them. You can use letters for this, and the holes in letters like P and D are especially useful. An anchoring point to attach to a bag, book or piece of work could be made from Ds, rather like the D-rings that are usually made of metal. An alternative would be to use patches, which could be folded over cords, or the cord or braid could be threaded through the patches.

As you will have seen from the ideas in this part of the book, the edges and the finishing techniques can be an exciting part of your work. Making edges, tassels and trimmings is great fun, too, so get stitching, use your imagination and enjoy yourself.

We hope that we have given you lots of ideas for stitching in layers. Go on to develop, experiment and change any or all of them as you try them out. Even if it is not very successful the first time, keep going, and you will make new discoveries and opportunities with your stitching.

Suppliers

SEWING MACHINES
Bernina, Bogod Machine Co. Ltd, 50–52 Great Sutton Street, London EC14 0DJ

Brother, Shepley Street, Audenshaw, Manchester M34 5JD

Husquvarna/Pfaff, Husquvarna Viking House, Cheddar Business Park, Wedmoor Road, Cheddar, Somerset BS27 3EB

Janome Centre, Southside, Bredbury, Stockport, Cheshire SK6 2SP

EQUIPMENT AND MATERIALS
Art Van Go, 16 Hollybush Lane, Datchworth, Knebworth, Herts SG3 6RE (heat guns, Xpandaprint, Markal oil sticks, masks, metal mesh, webbing, webbing spray, wireform and acrylic wax)

Inca Studio, 10 Duke Street, Princes Risborough, Bucks HP27 0AT (Kunin felt, water-soluble fabric and paper, 505 spray)

International Sewing Notions, 3 Townhead Terrace, Paisley, Renfrew PA1 2AU

Oliver Twists, 34 Holmlands Park, Chester-Le-Street, Co Durham DH3 3PJ. (Metal shim, machine embroidery threads)

Rainbow Silks, 6 Wheelers Yard, High Street, Great Missenden, Bucks HP16 0AL (fabrics, paints, webbing, 505 spray)

Strata, Oronsay, Misbourne Avenue, Chalfont St Peter, Bucks SL9 0PF (Xpandaprint, chiffons, thermoplastic foam (softsculpt))

Winifred Cottage, 17 Elms Road, Fleet, Hants GU13 9EG (variegated threads, water-soluble paper)

Fabrics
Whaleys (Bradford) Ltd, Harris Court Road, Great Horton, Bradford, West Yorkshire BD7 4EQ

Threads
Silken Strands, 20 Y Rhos, Bangor, LL57 2LT (machine embroidery threads)

T.C. Threads Ltd, Unit 1, Benneworth Close, Hucknell, Nottingham, Notts NG15 6EL

USA
Most materials used in the book are available from art shops, but specifically:

Dick Blick Art Materials (Mail Order) 1-800-447-8192 (general art materials, including Shiva (Markal) oil sticks)

Gerber EZ-Liner Diaper Liners 1-800-4-GERBER

Australia
The Thread Studio, 6 Smith Street, Perth, WA 6000, Australia, tel. +61 89227 1561 (full range of art and embroidery supplies)

New Zealand
Craft Supplies, 31 Gurney Road, Belmont, Lower Hutt, New Zealand, tel. +644 565 0544.

Index